VERTEX

© DARKK ERA 2020

Photographs and design by Jarod Gibson
Editing by Claudia Tavernese

All rights reserved. No portion of this work
may be reproduced, stored in a retrieval system,
or transmitted in any form or by any means,
mechanical, electronic, photocopying,
recording, or otherwise, without written permission
from the author.

DARKK ERA
www.darkk.ca
www.darkk.bandcamp.com
www.instagram.com/darkkera__
www.facebook.com/darkk.era.ca

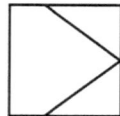

ISBN 978-1-716-65598-2

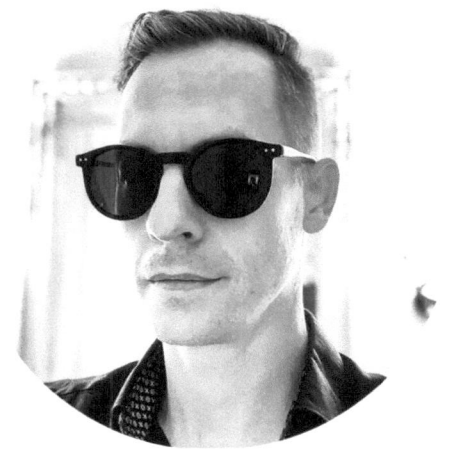

V E R T E X

These photographs were taken between 2015 and 2018. I specifically removed the standard context of the buildings by framing them as minimal geometric shapes against the skies they filled. Sometimes the structure itself was interesting enough, but other times, by mirroring or rotating, an even more monolithic, otherworldly image was found. The typical perspective —simply looking up—could transform into one that was new and impossible, but still realistic.

Jarod Gibson
Toronto, Canada
July 2020

SPECIAL THANKS TO

Claudia Tavernese, Brenda and Alan Trieber, Gerry and Jeanne Gibson, Deb and Grant Carl, Colleen Gibson, Daren Williams, Andrea Rothecker, Kristy Gibson, Alyssa Gibson, Maddison Williams, Luca Tavernese, and Louie Tavernese.

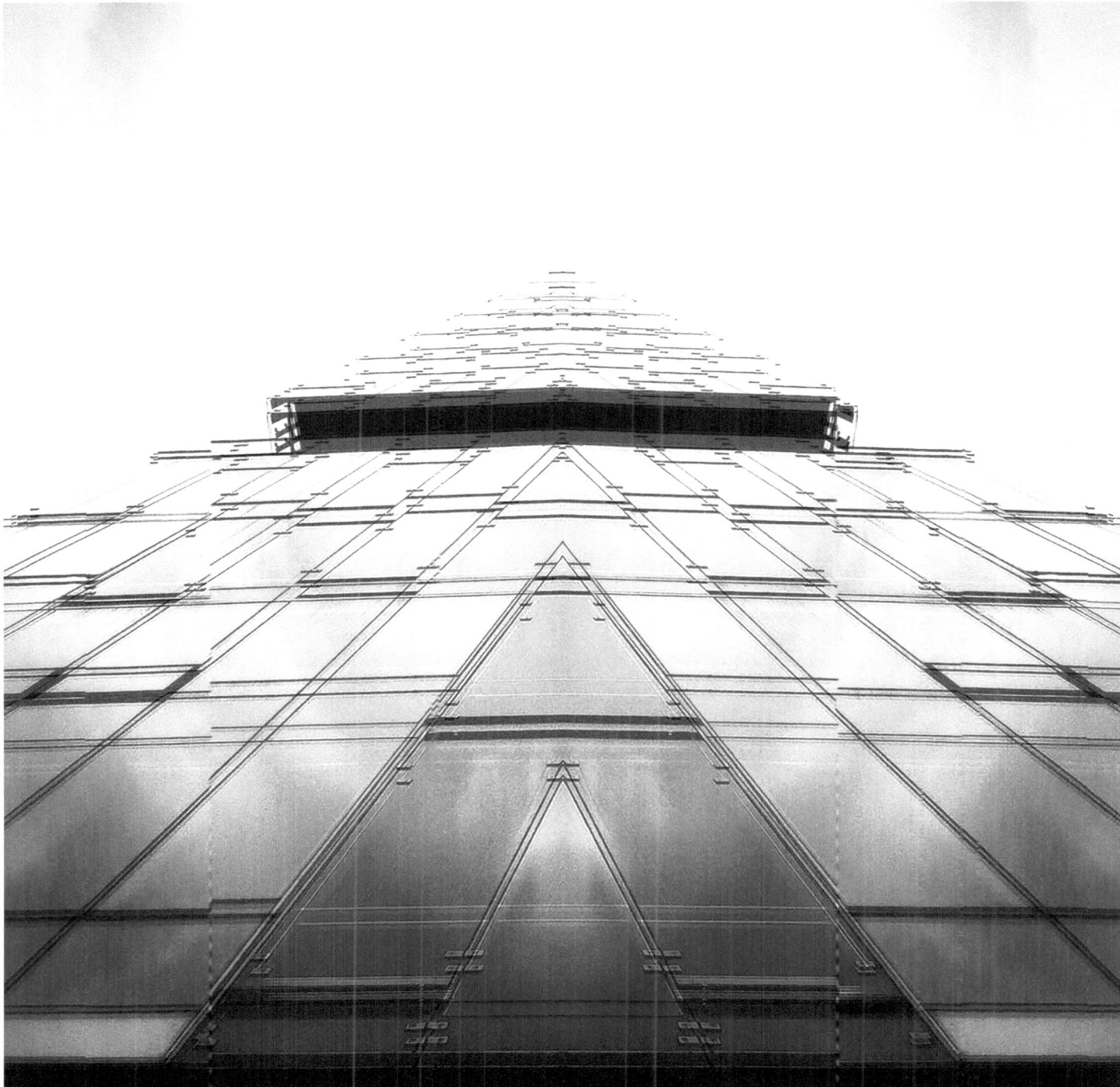

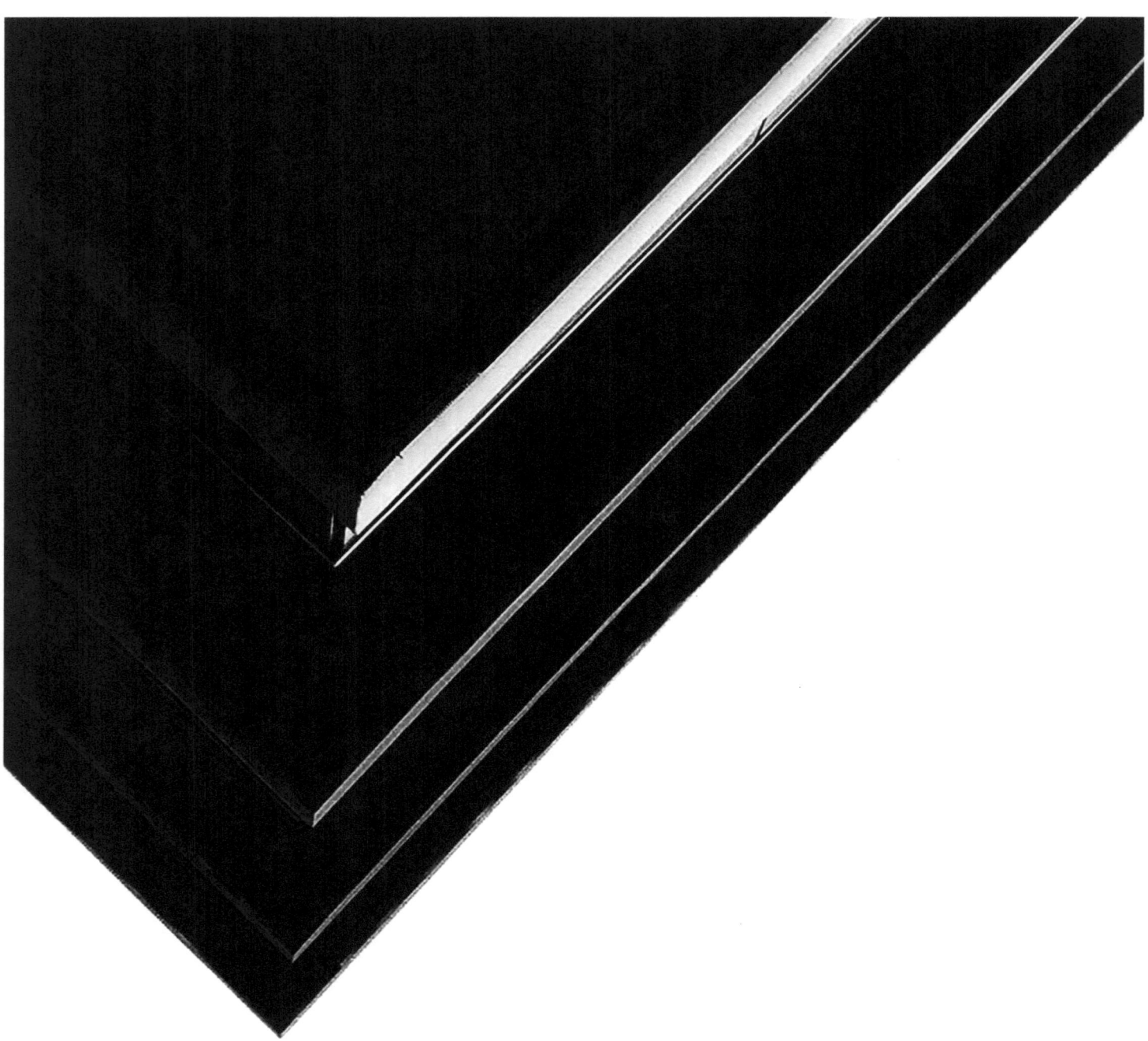

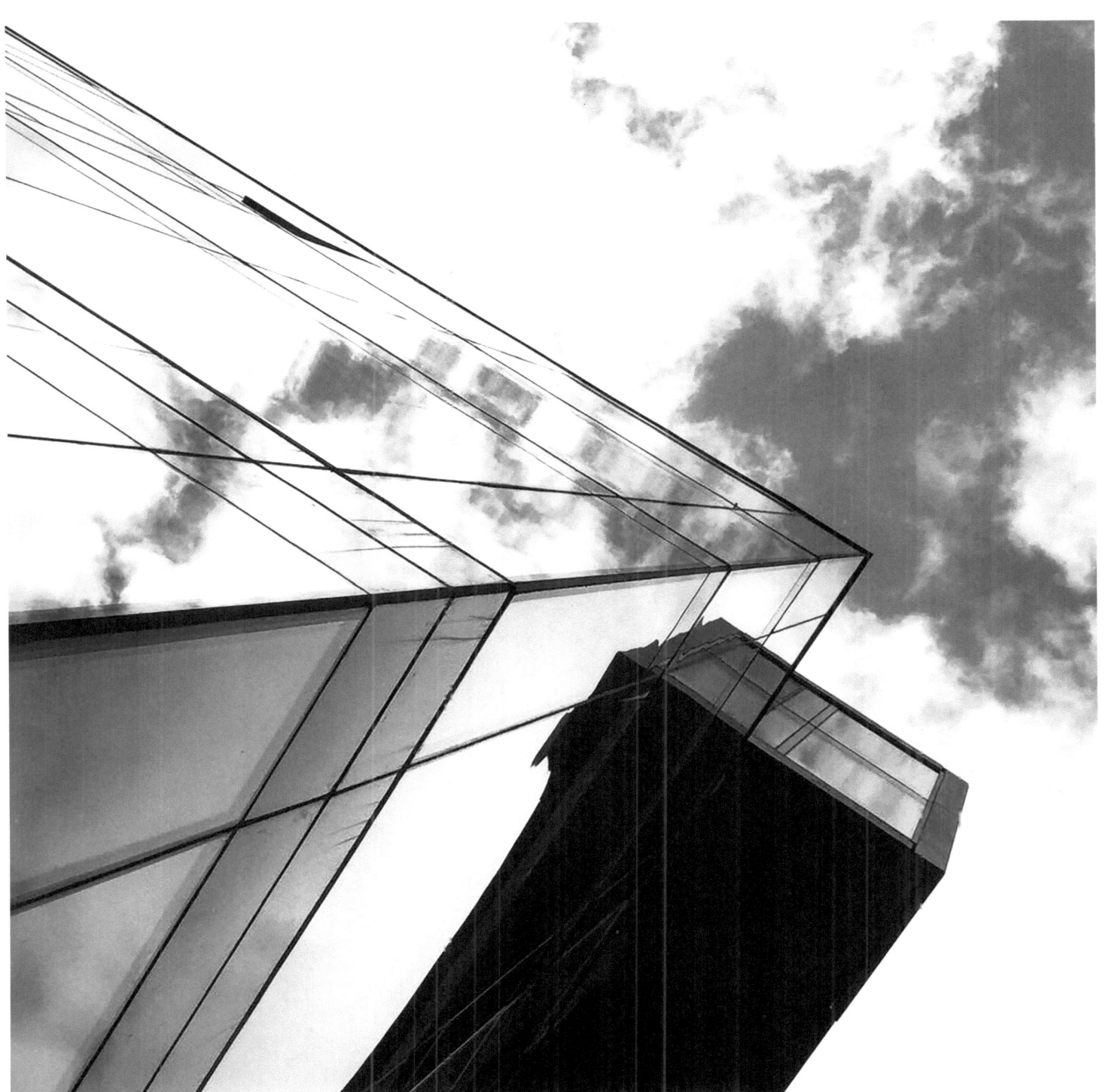

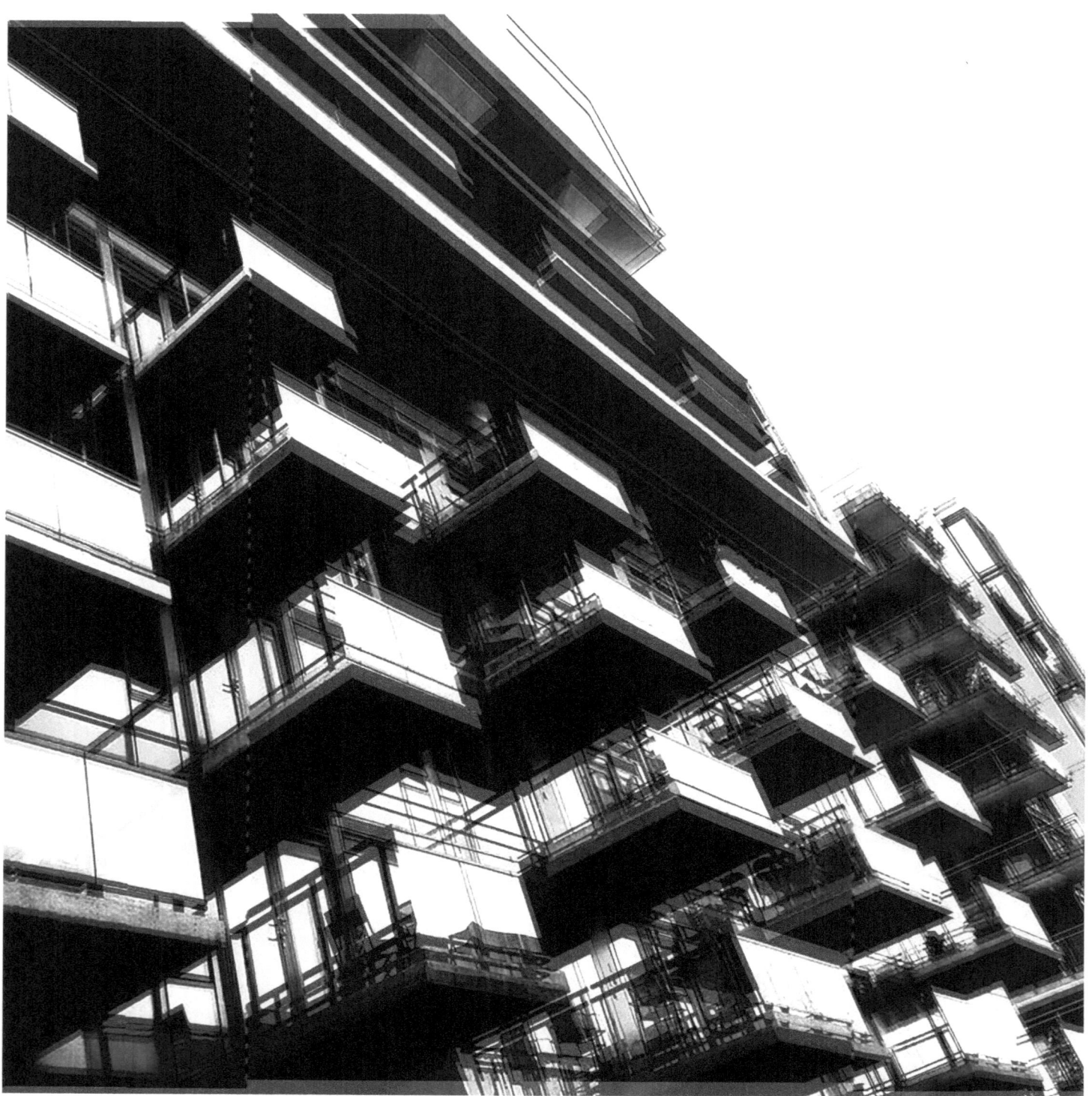

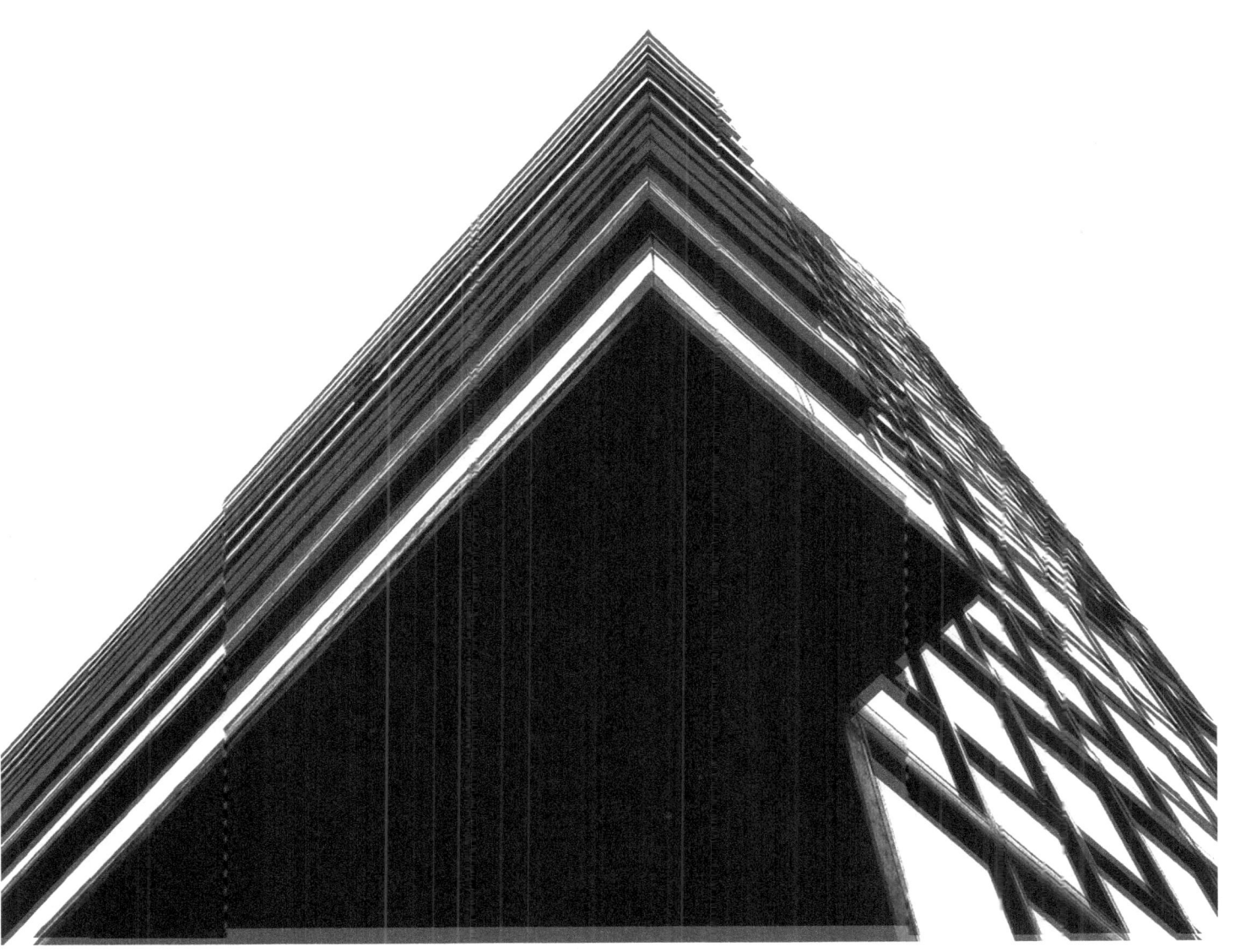

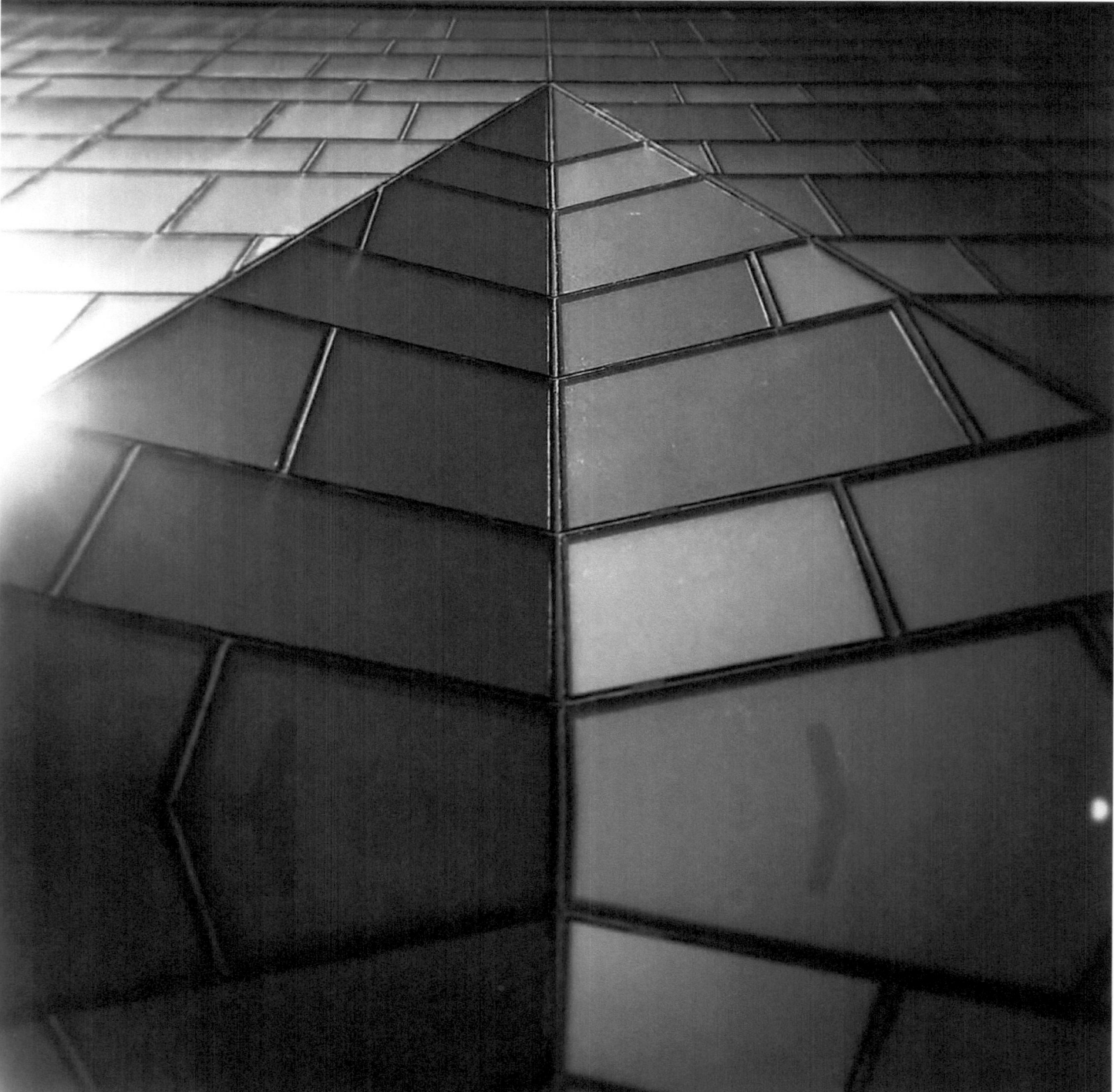

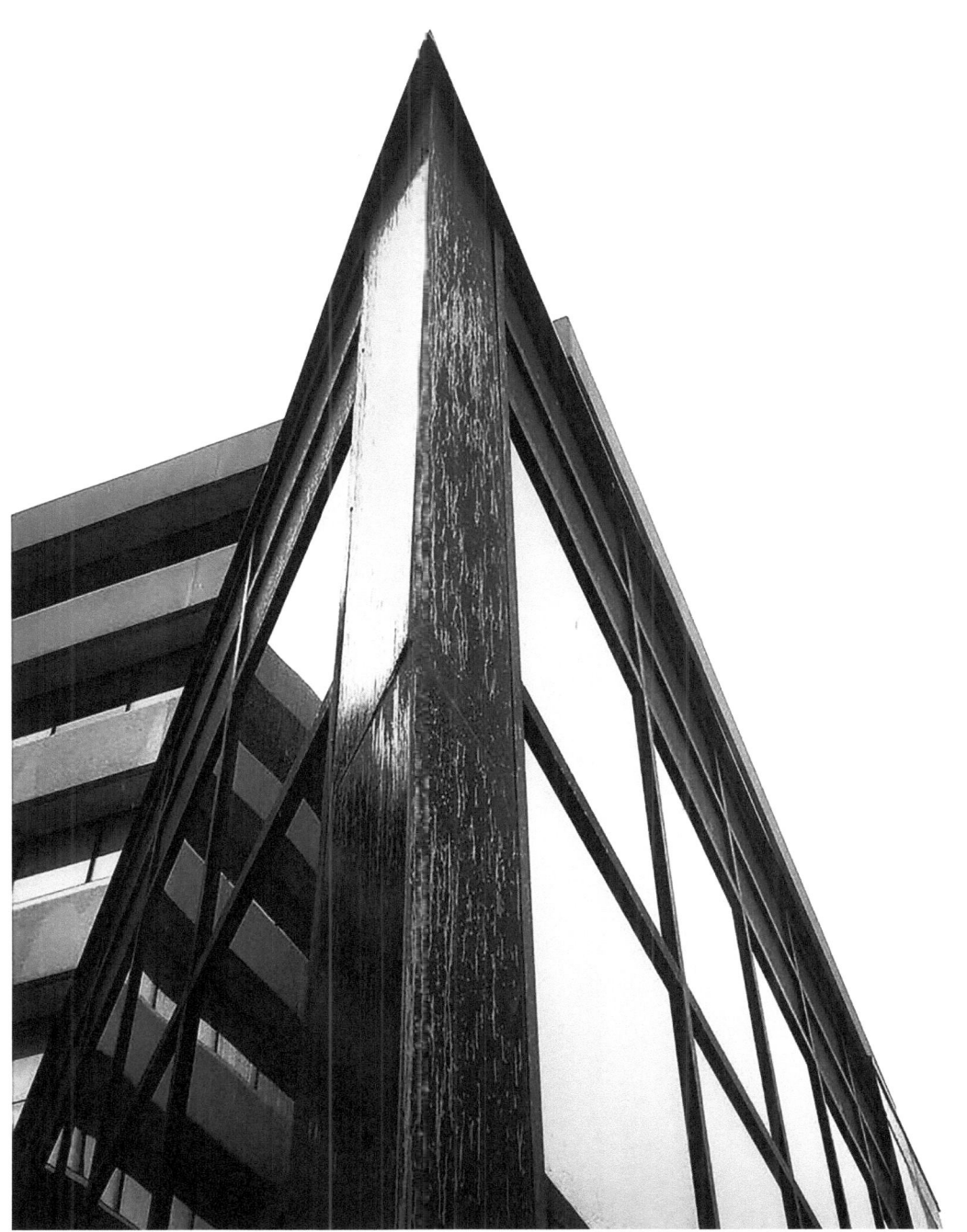

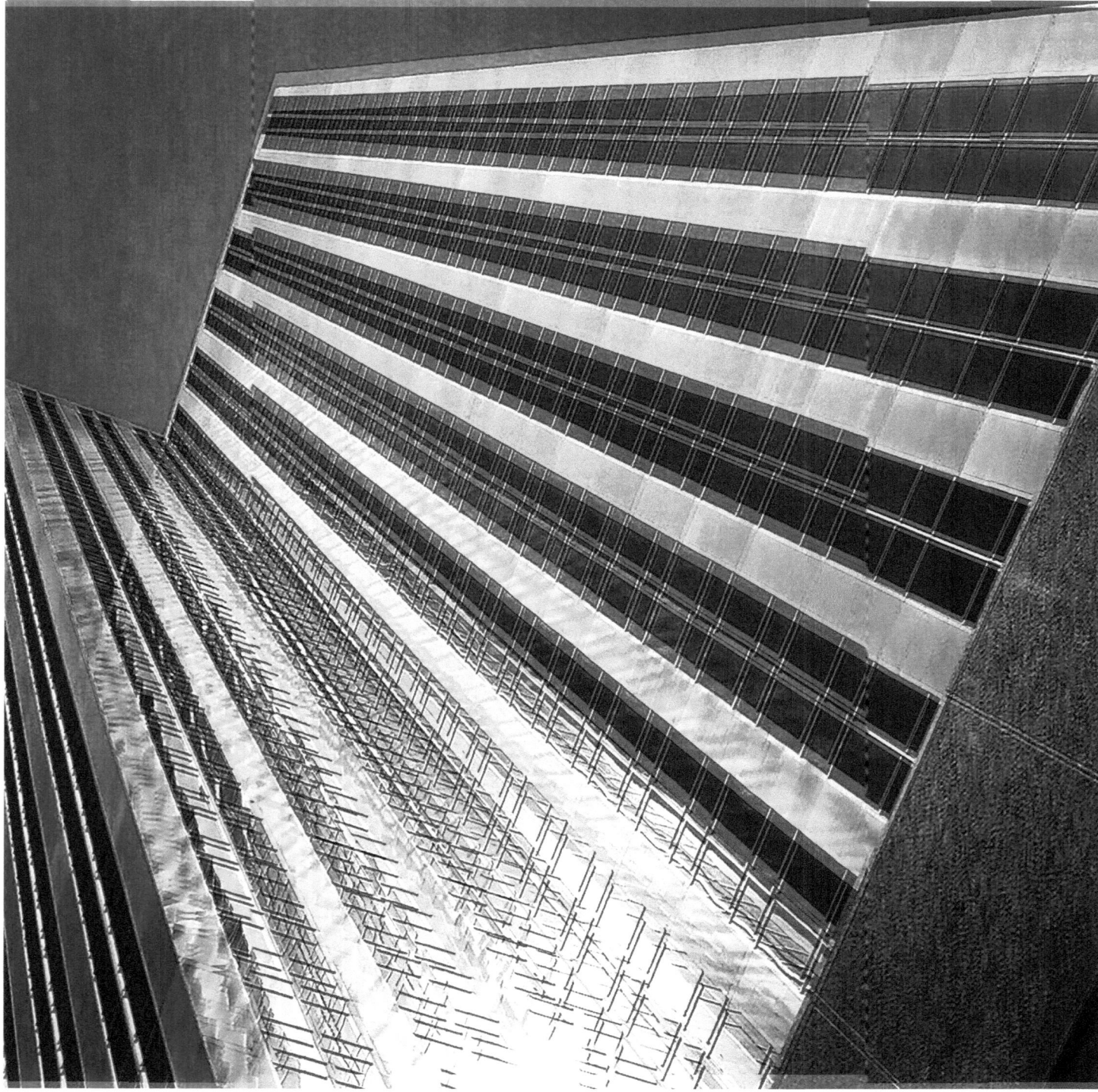

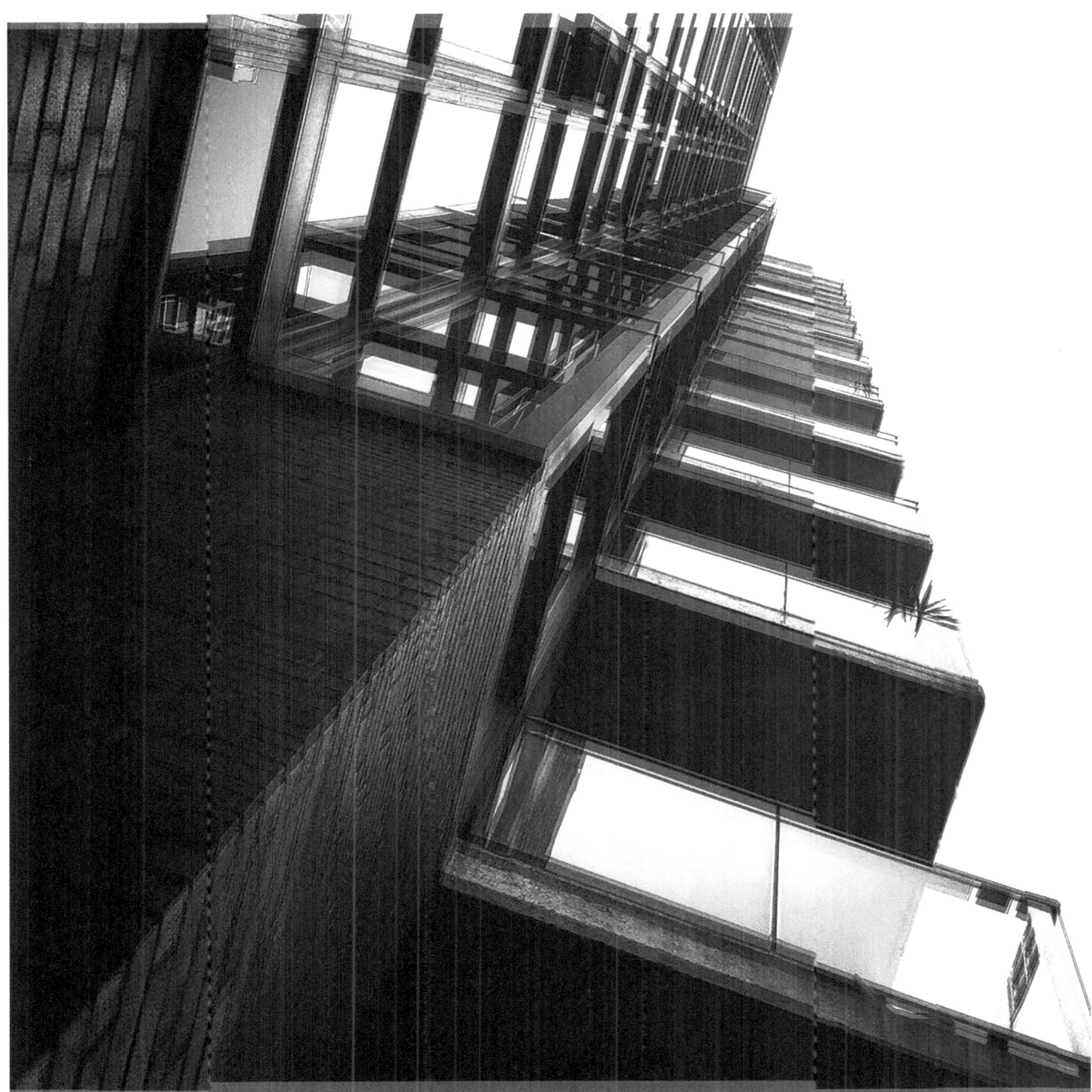

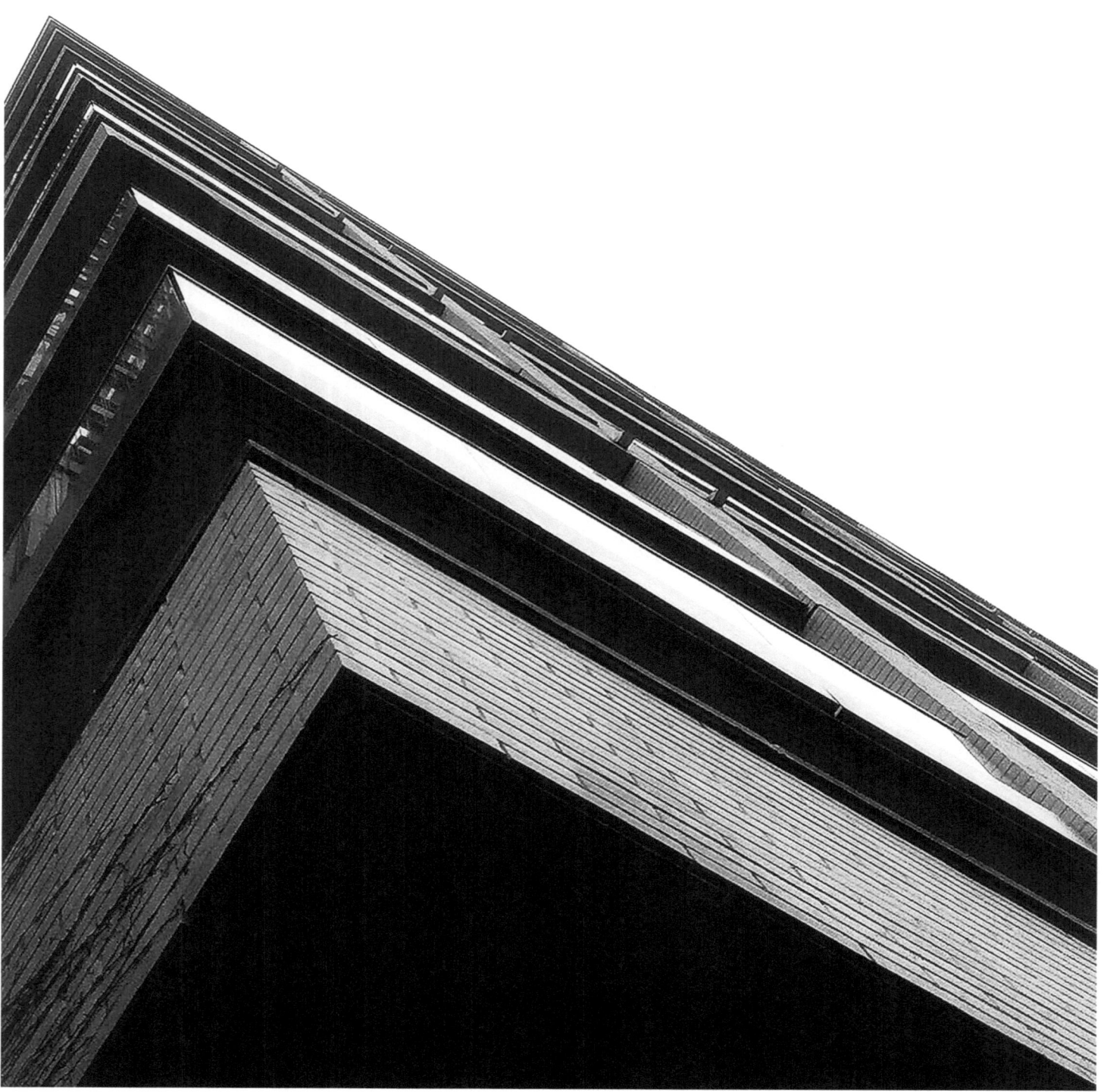

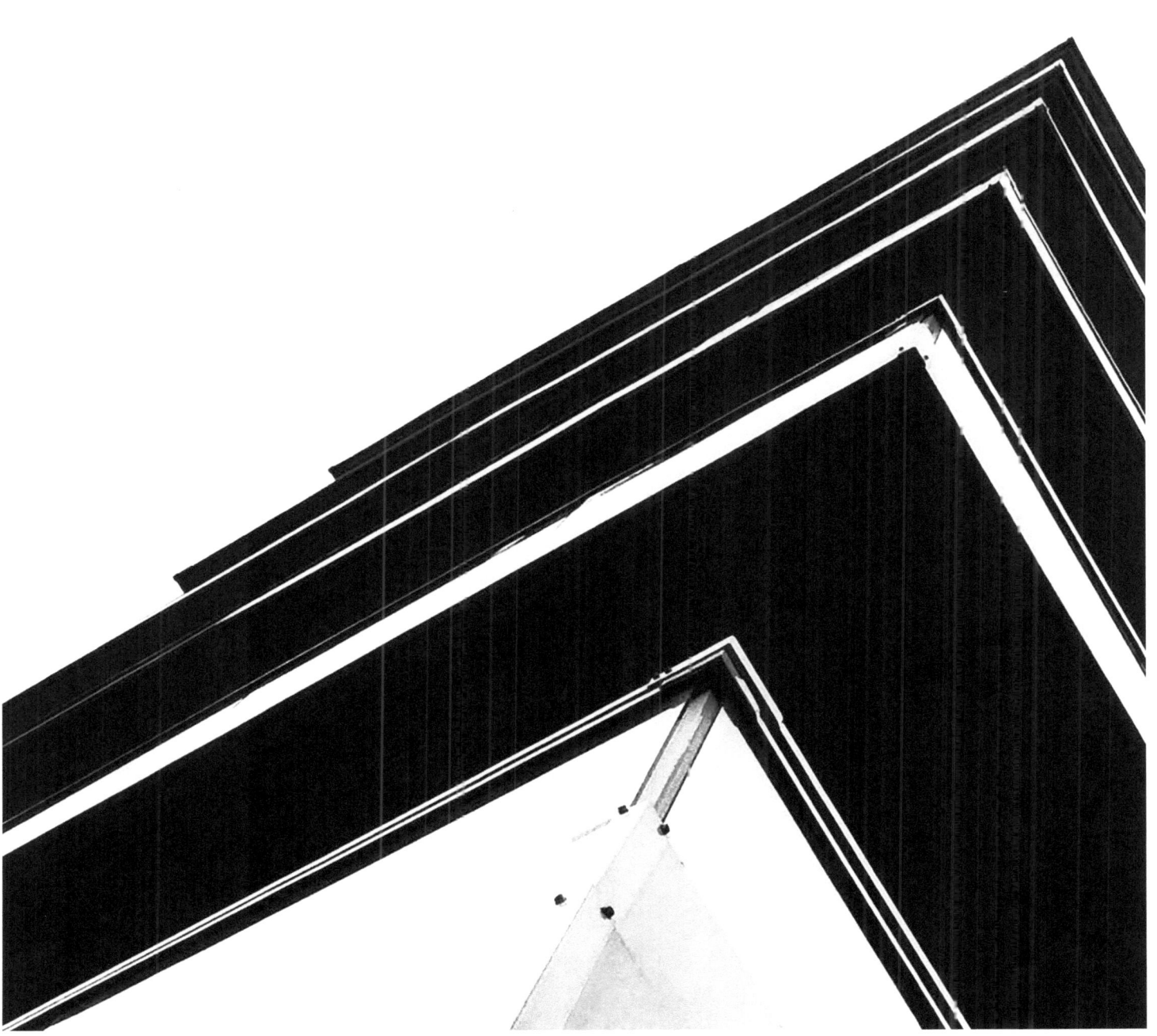

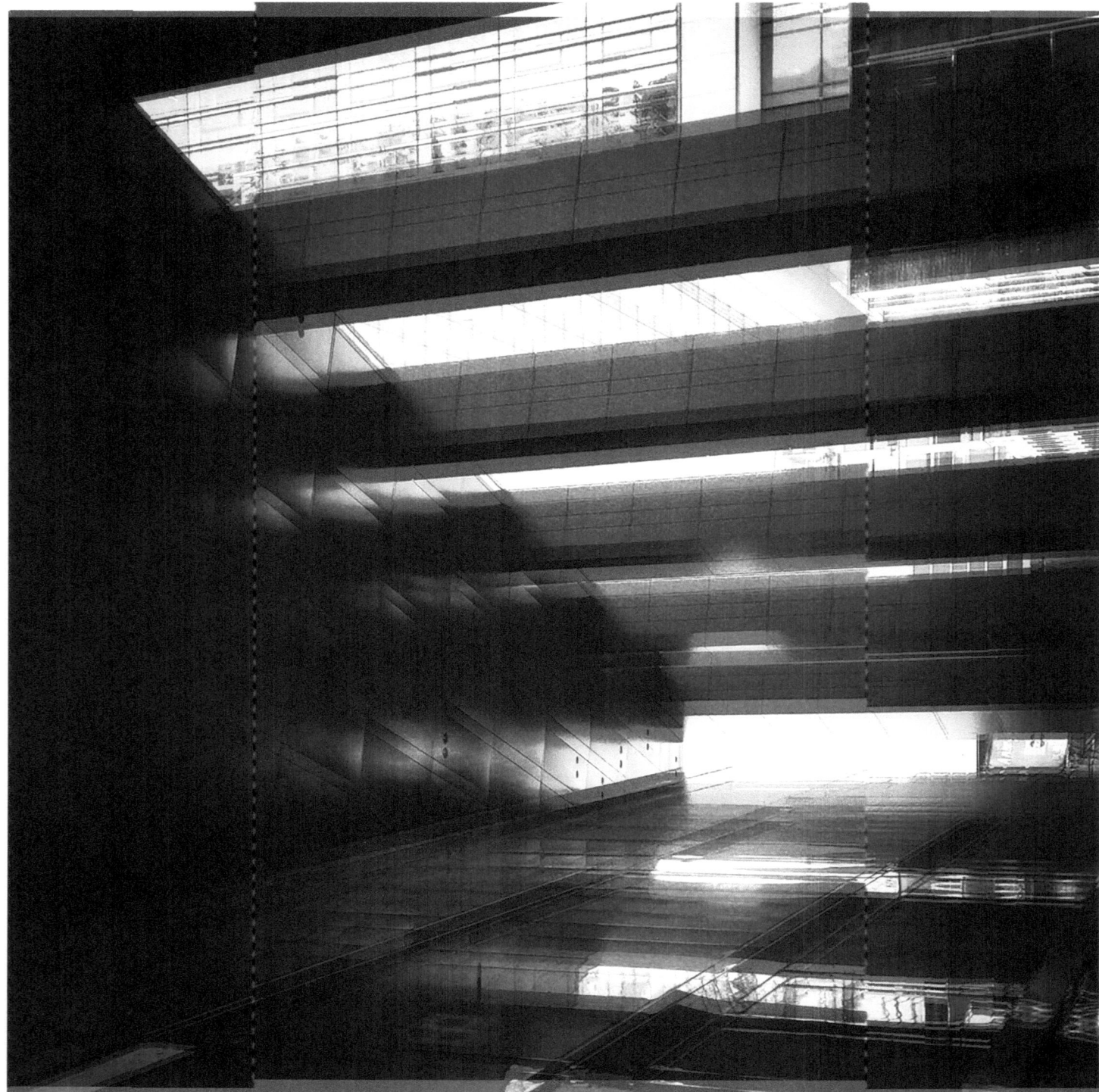

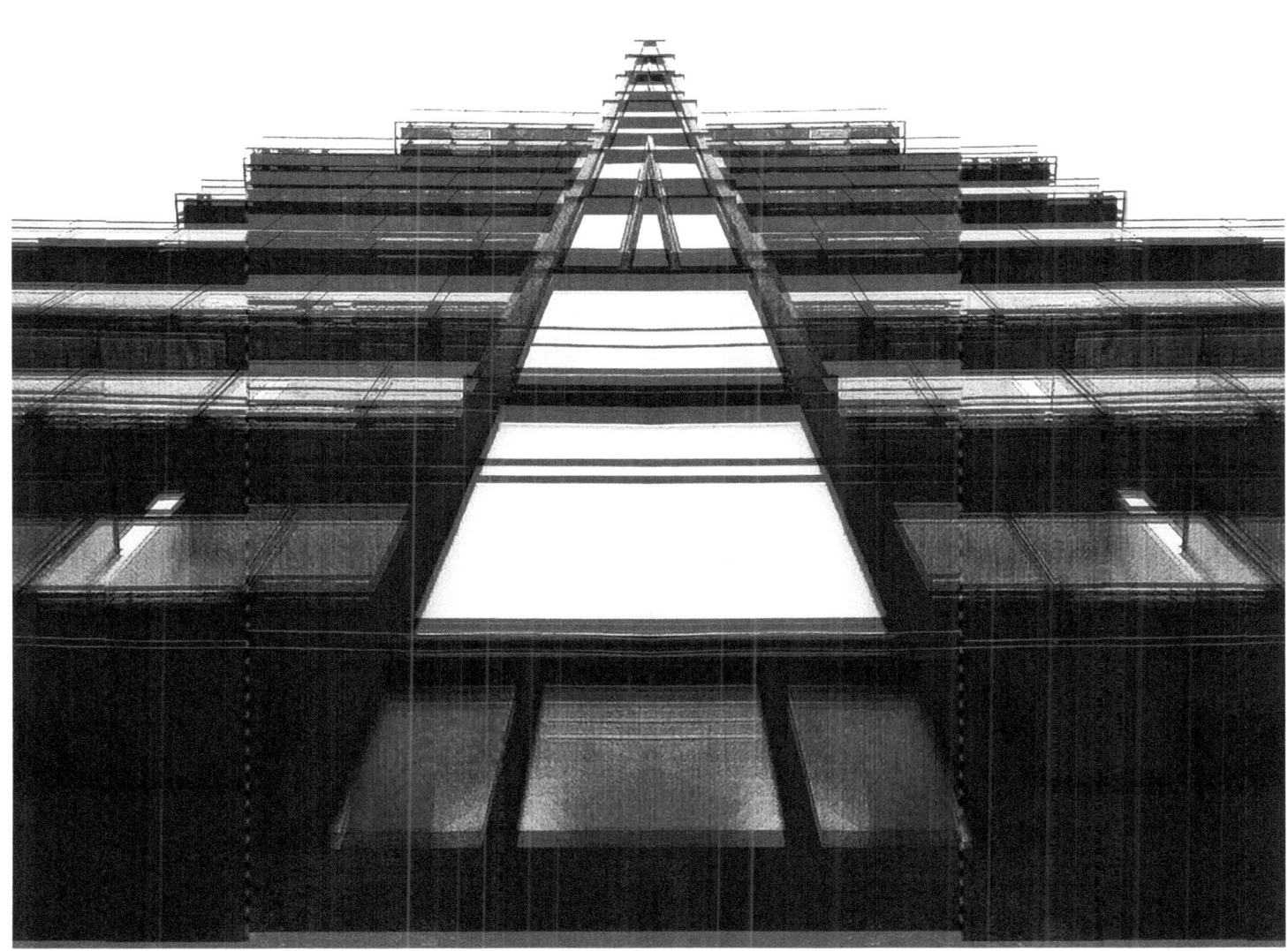

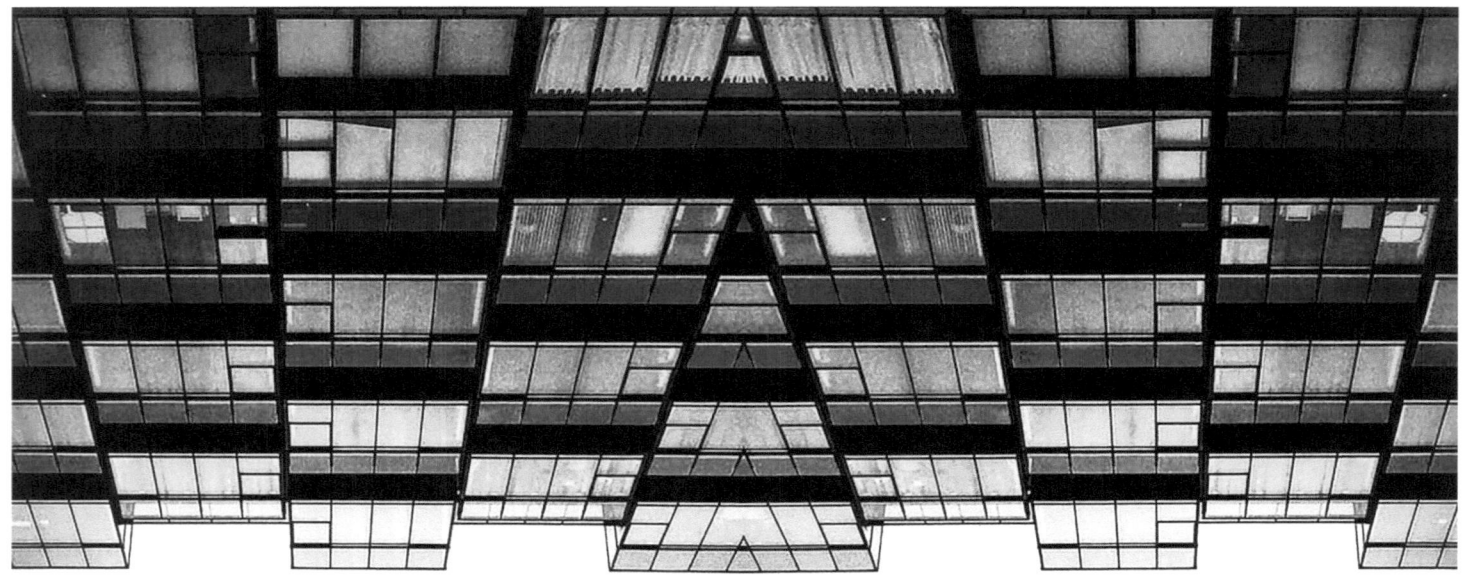

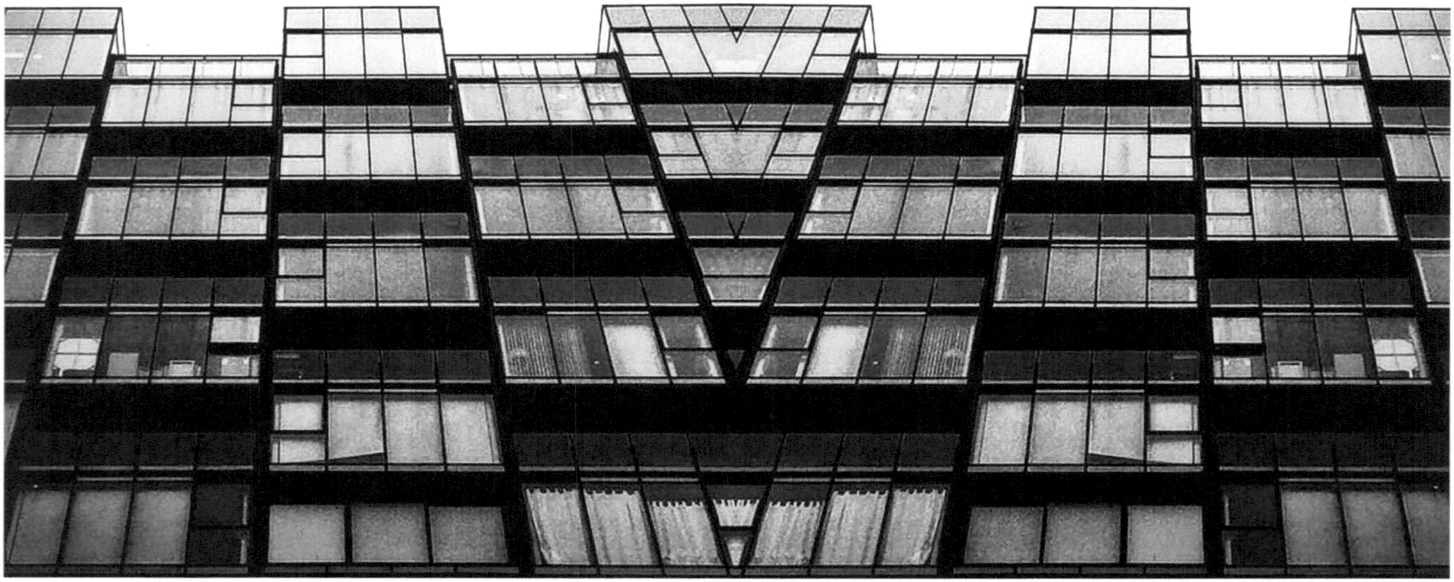

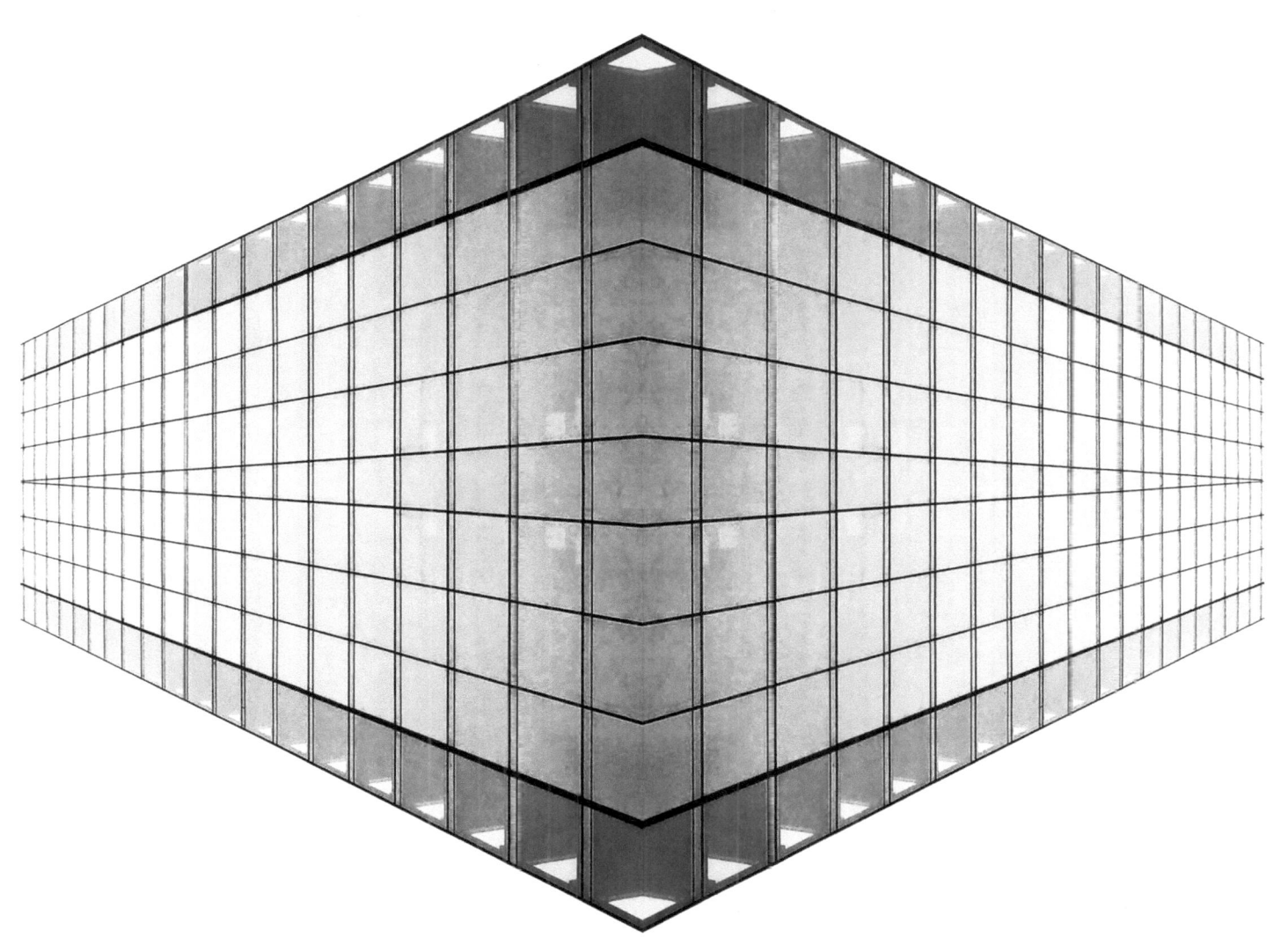

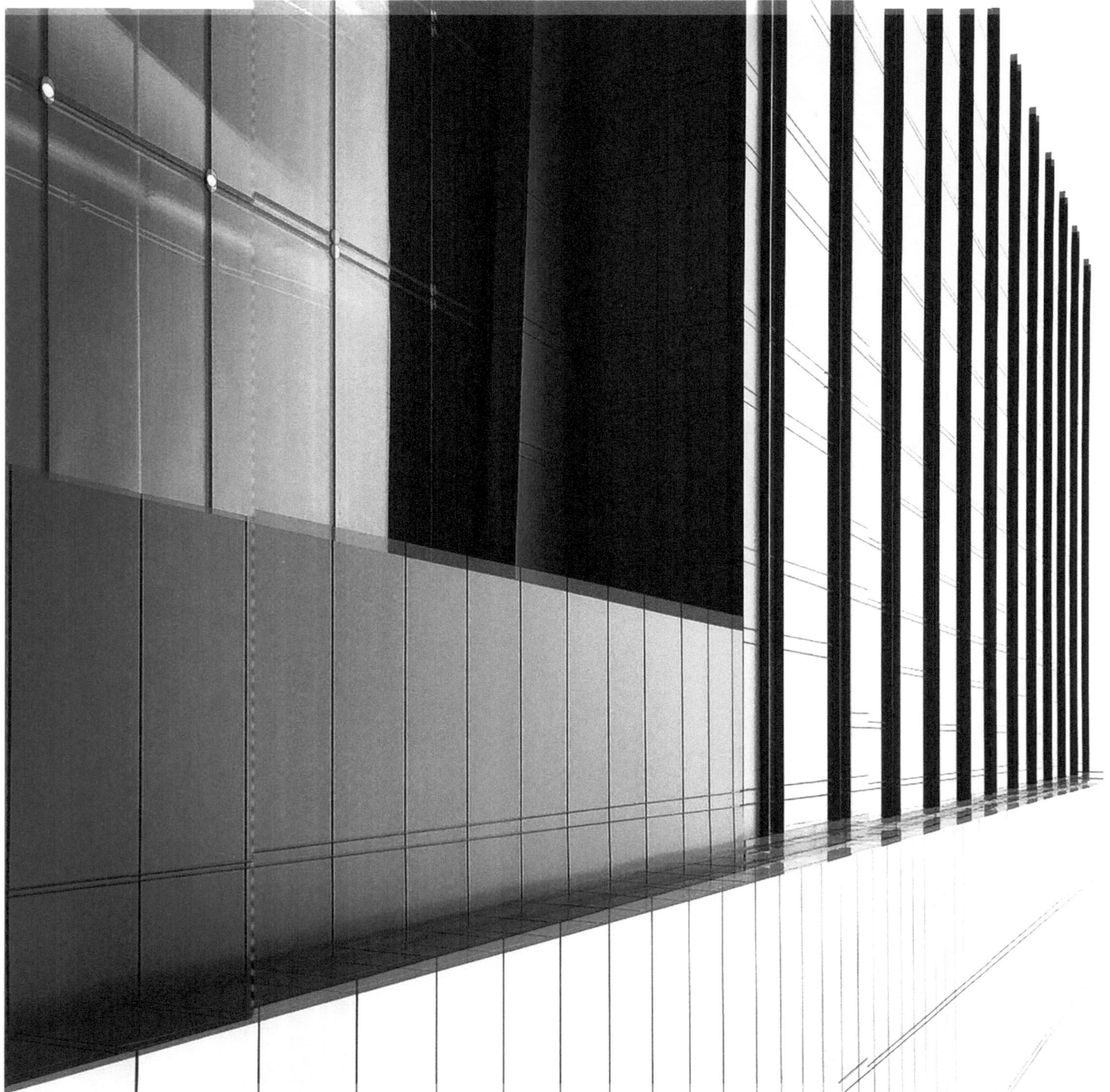

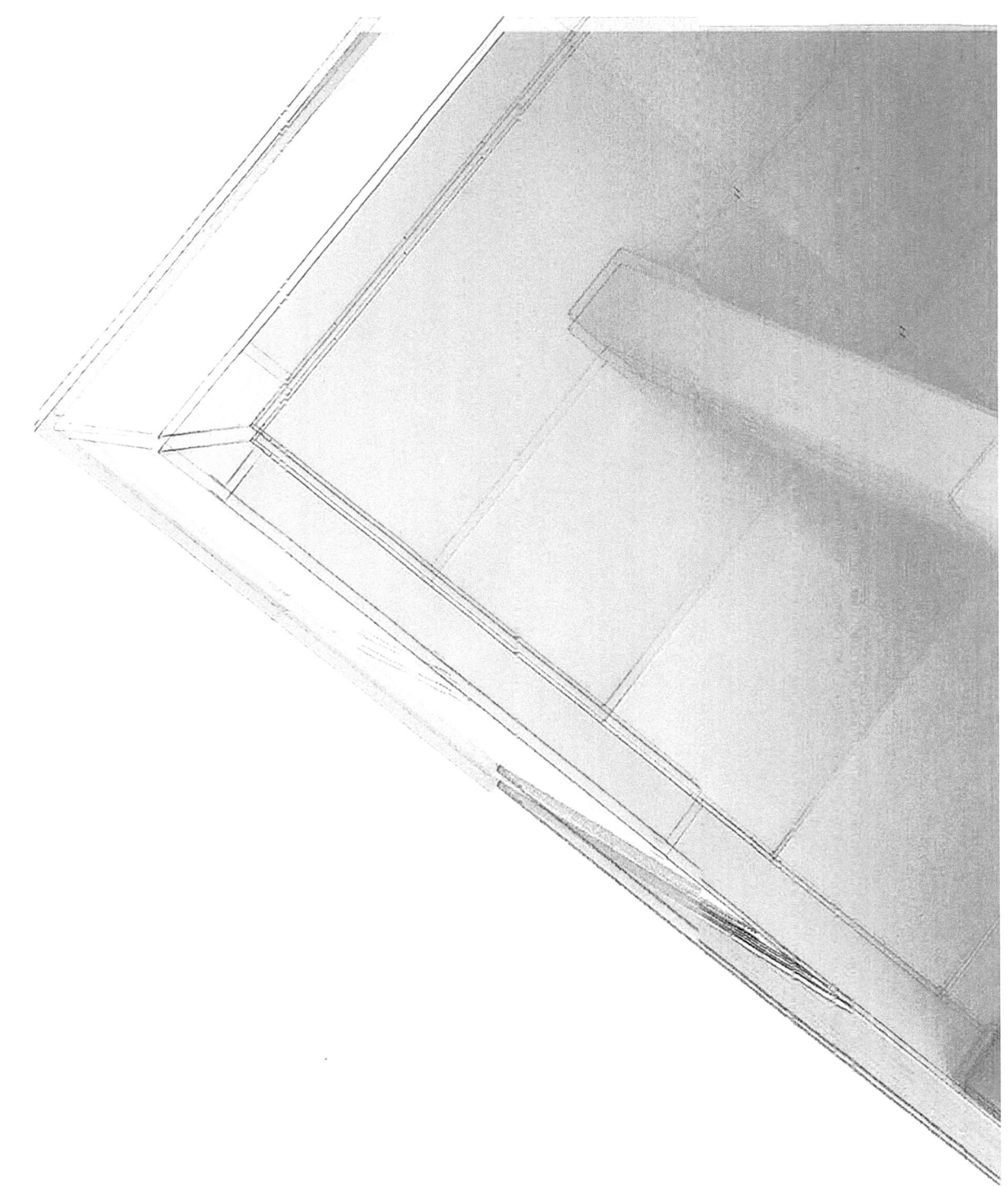

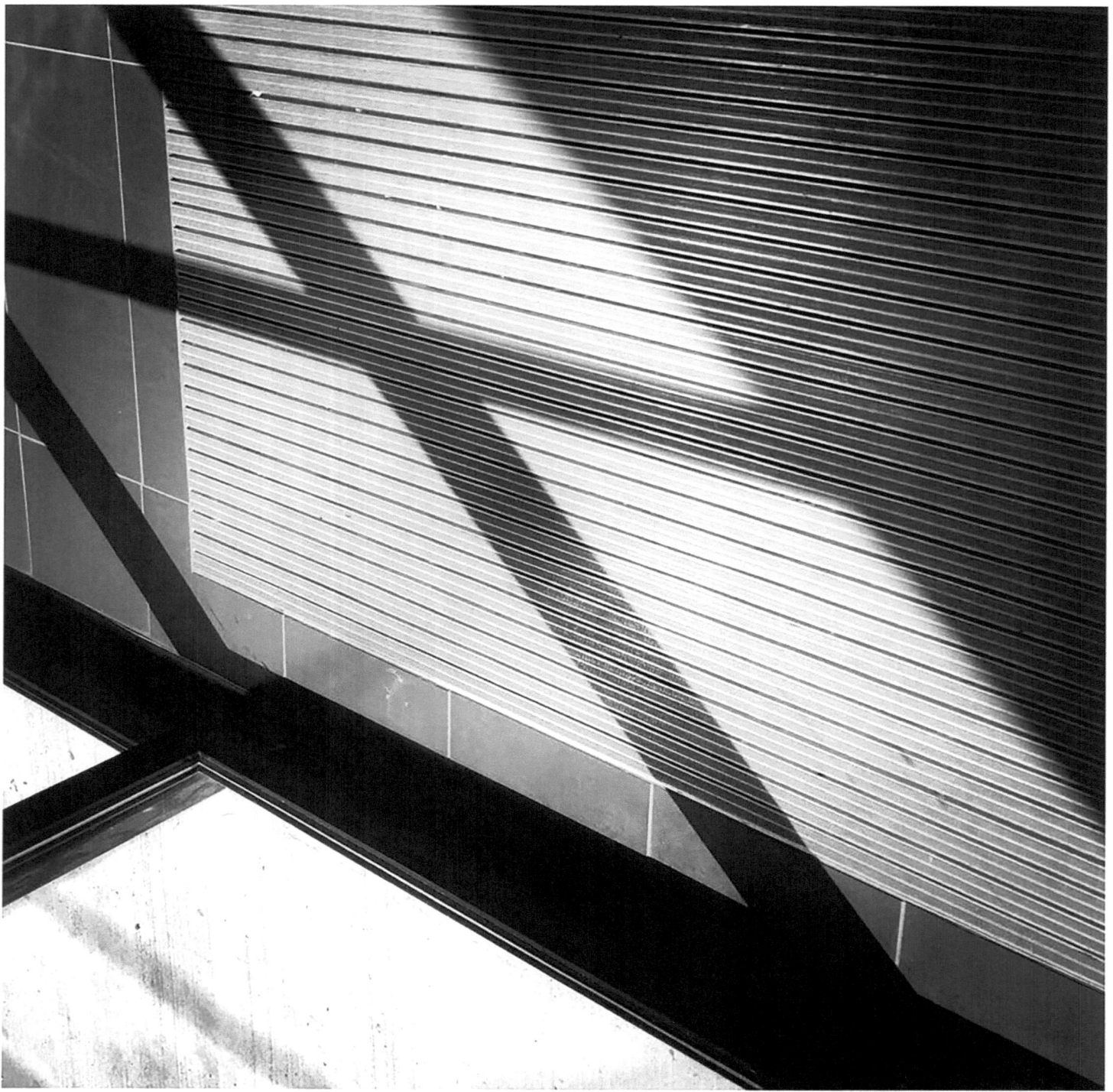

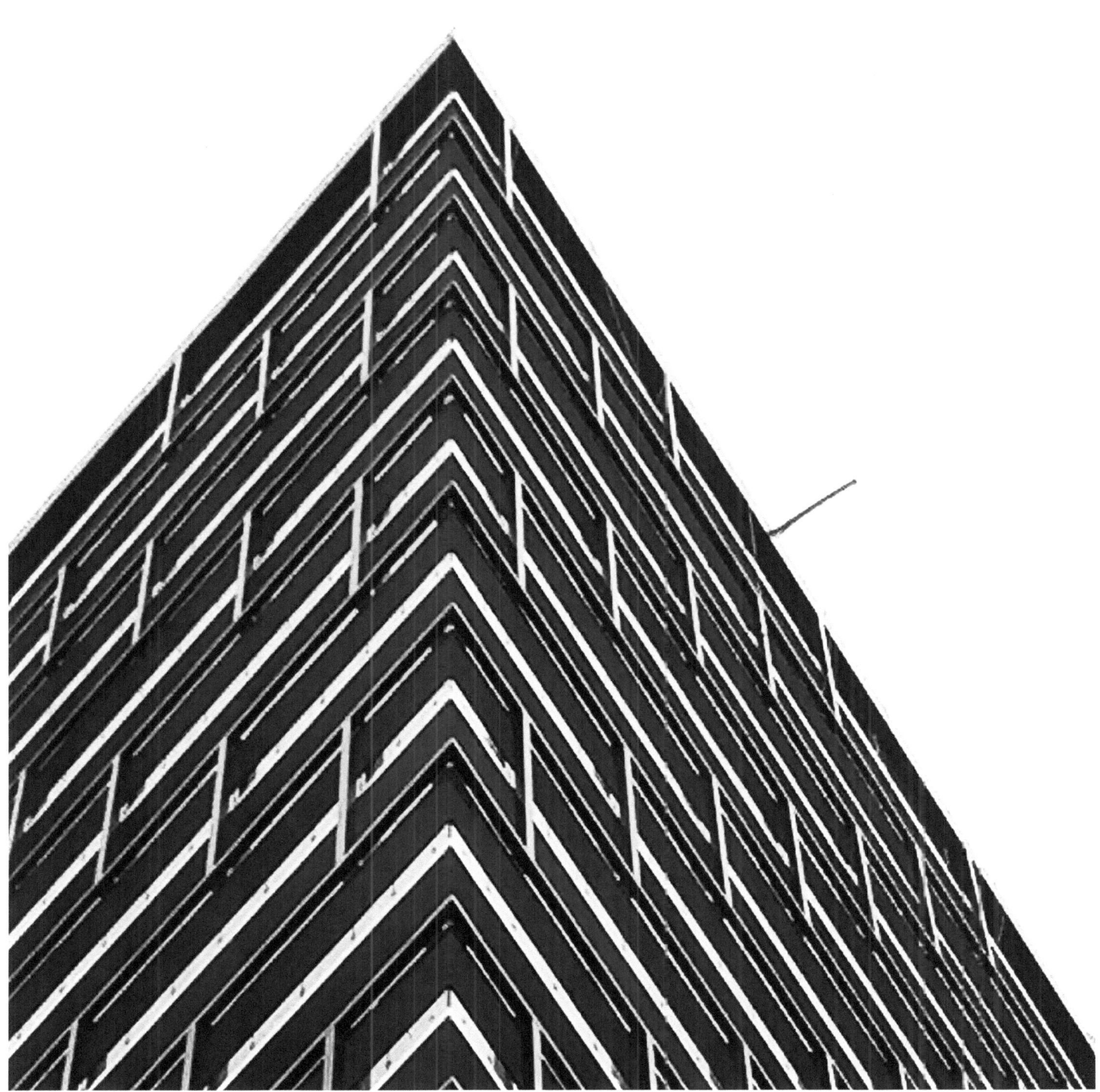

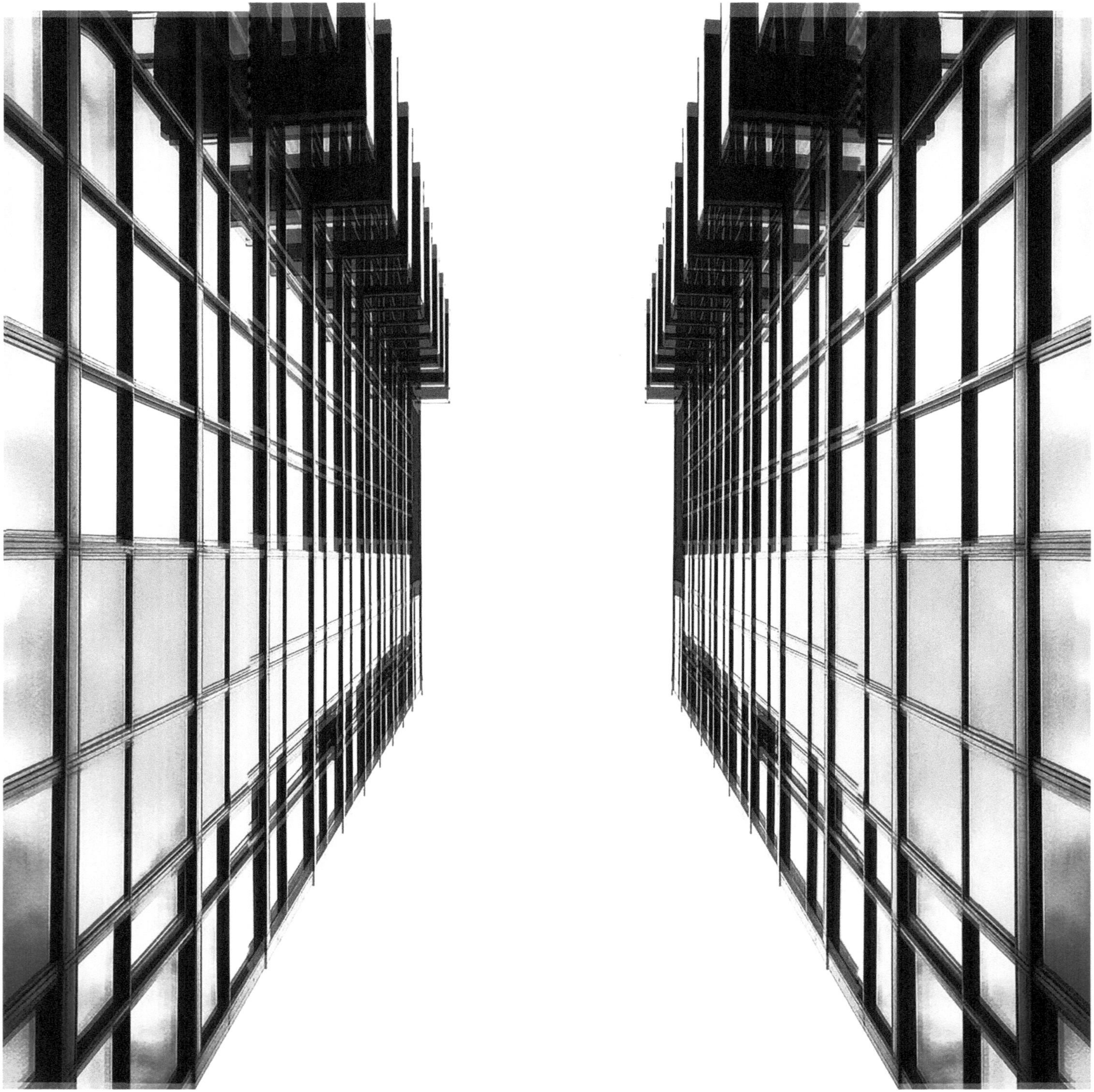

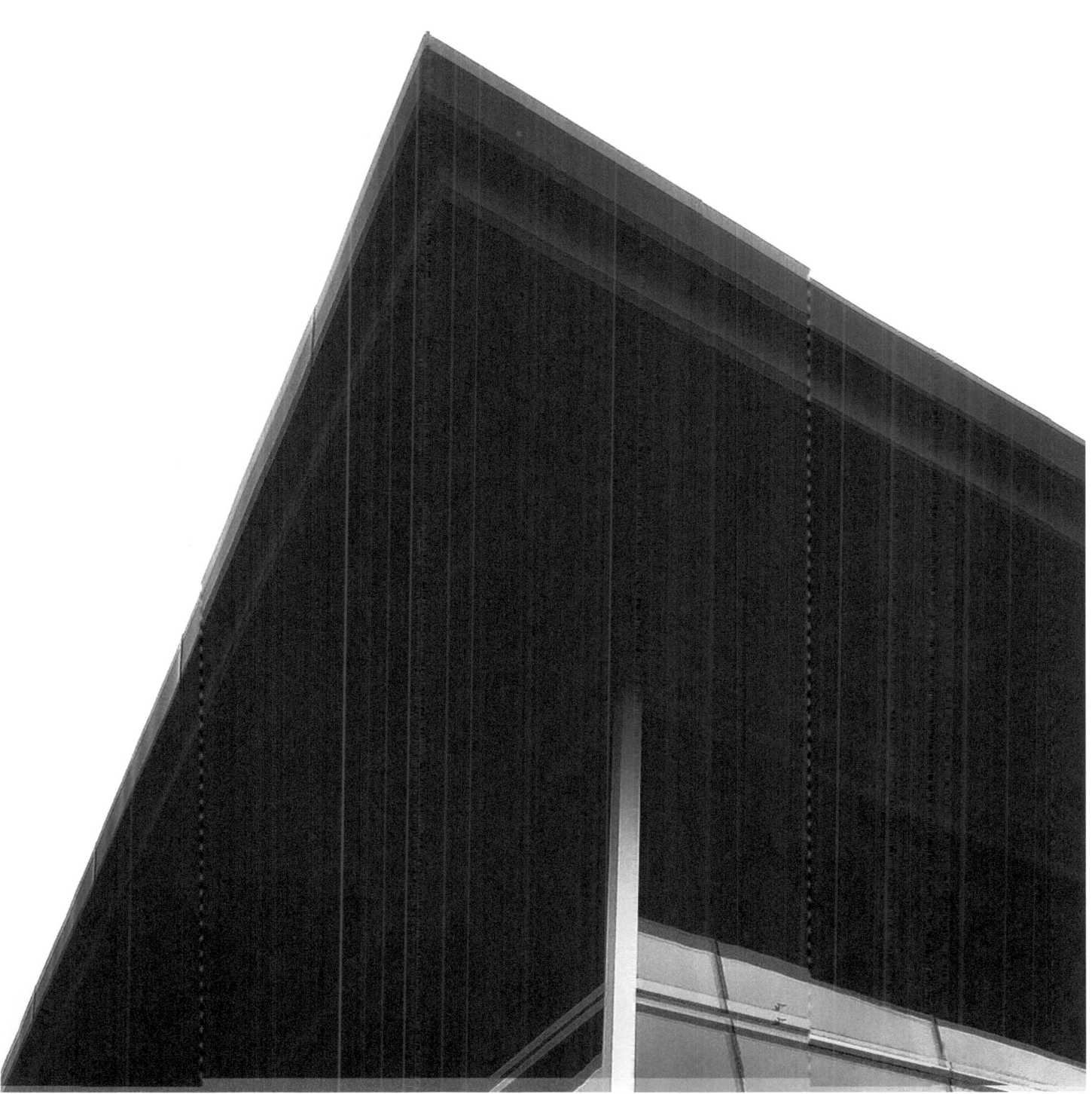

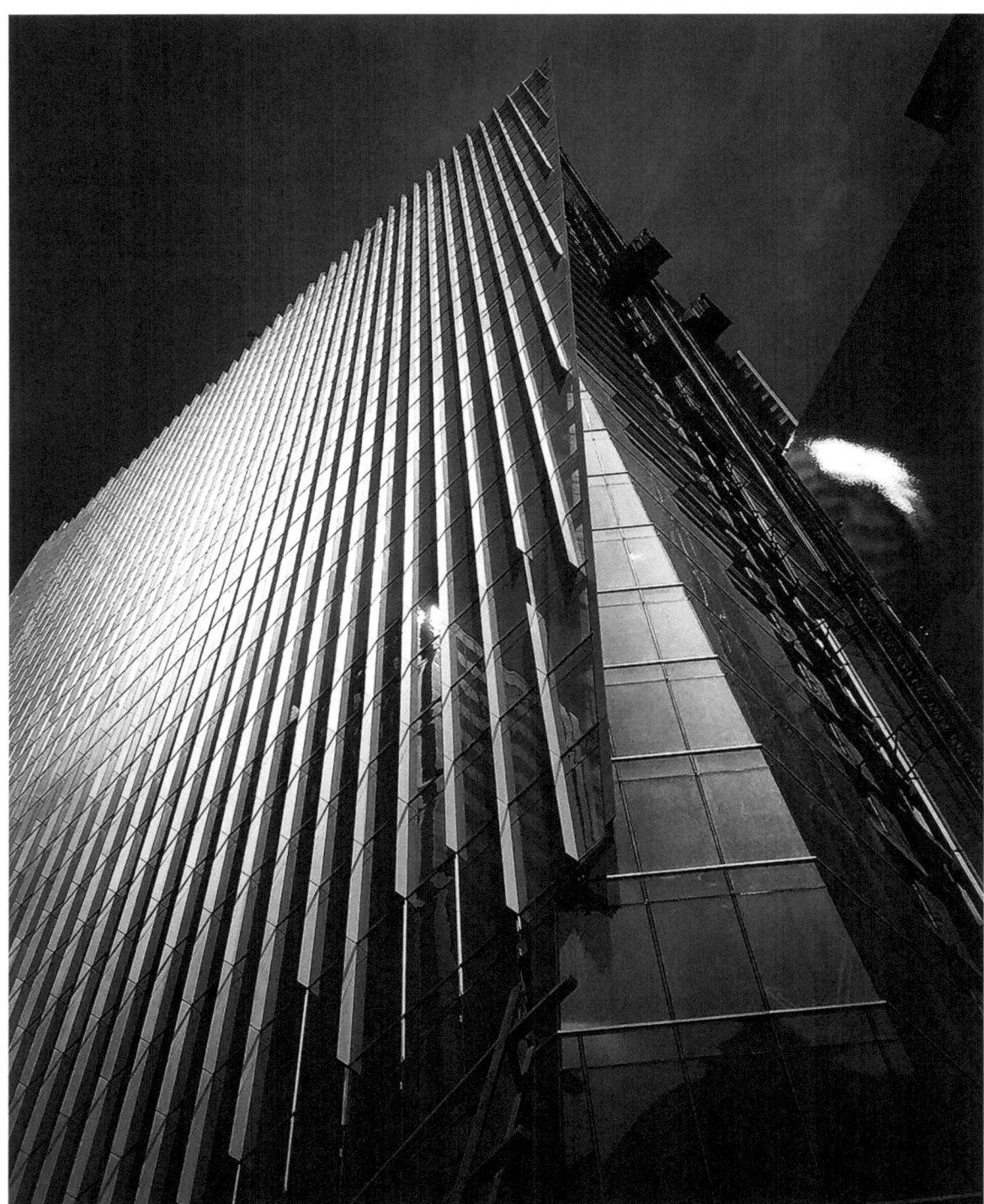

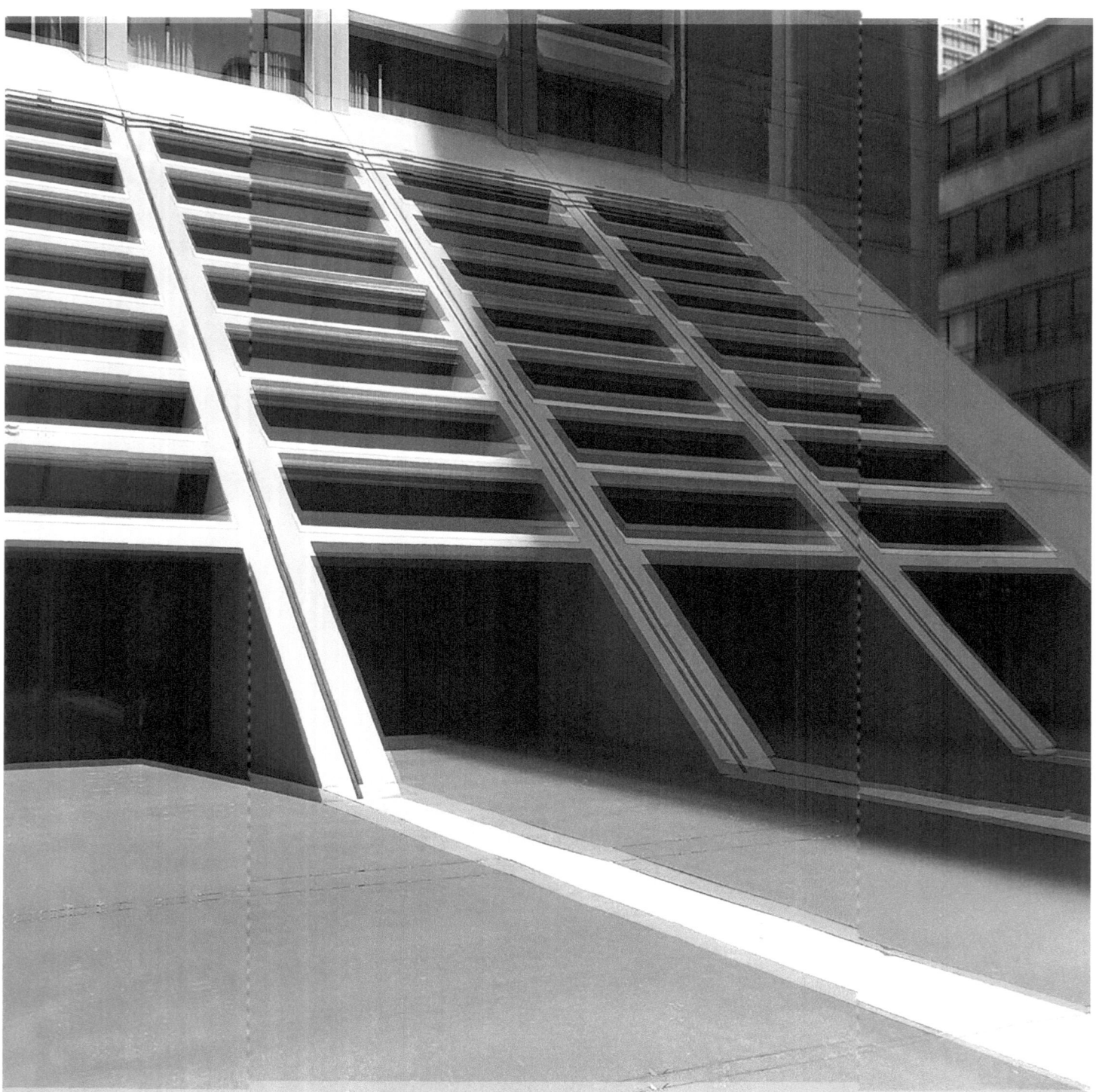

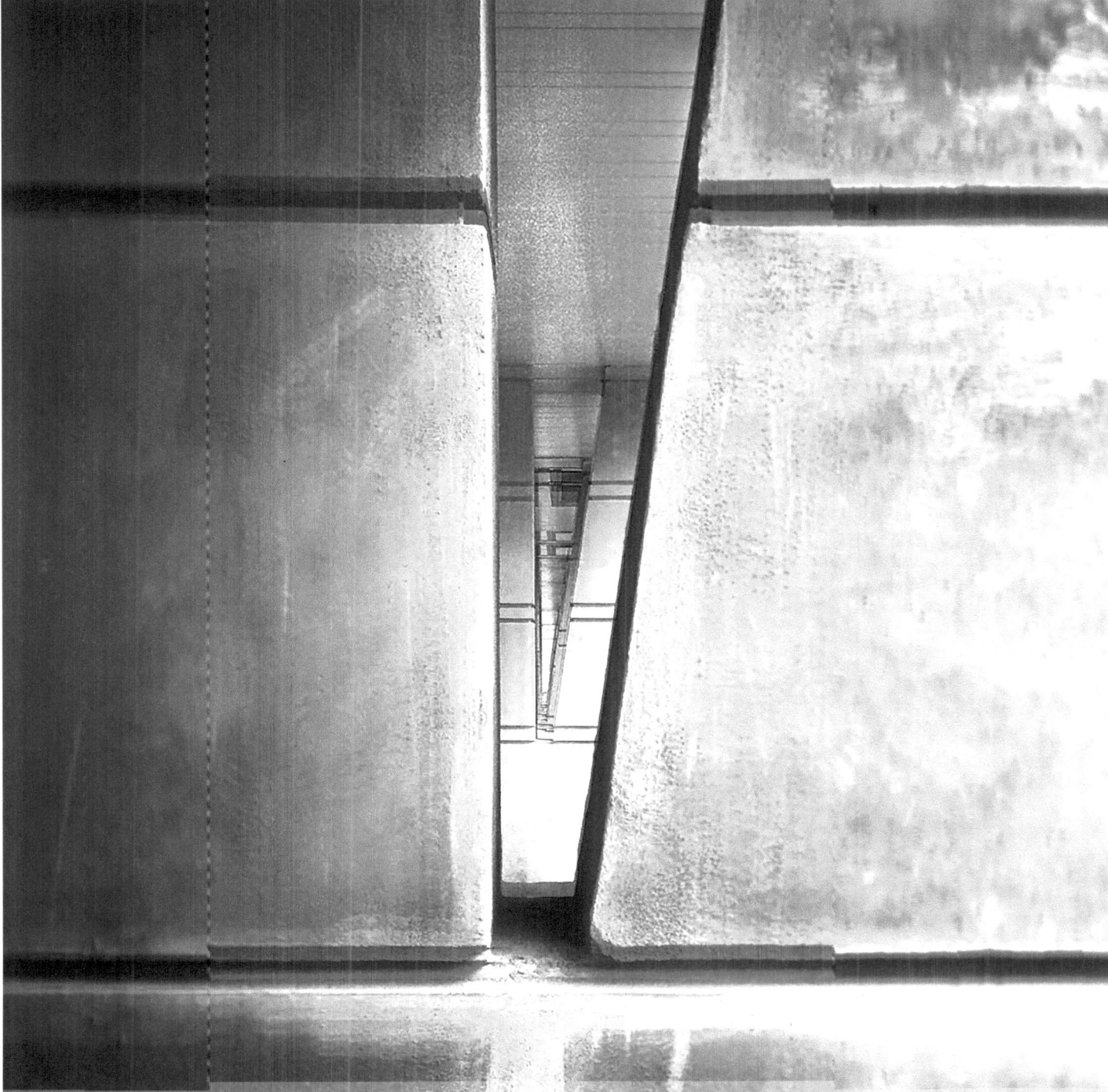

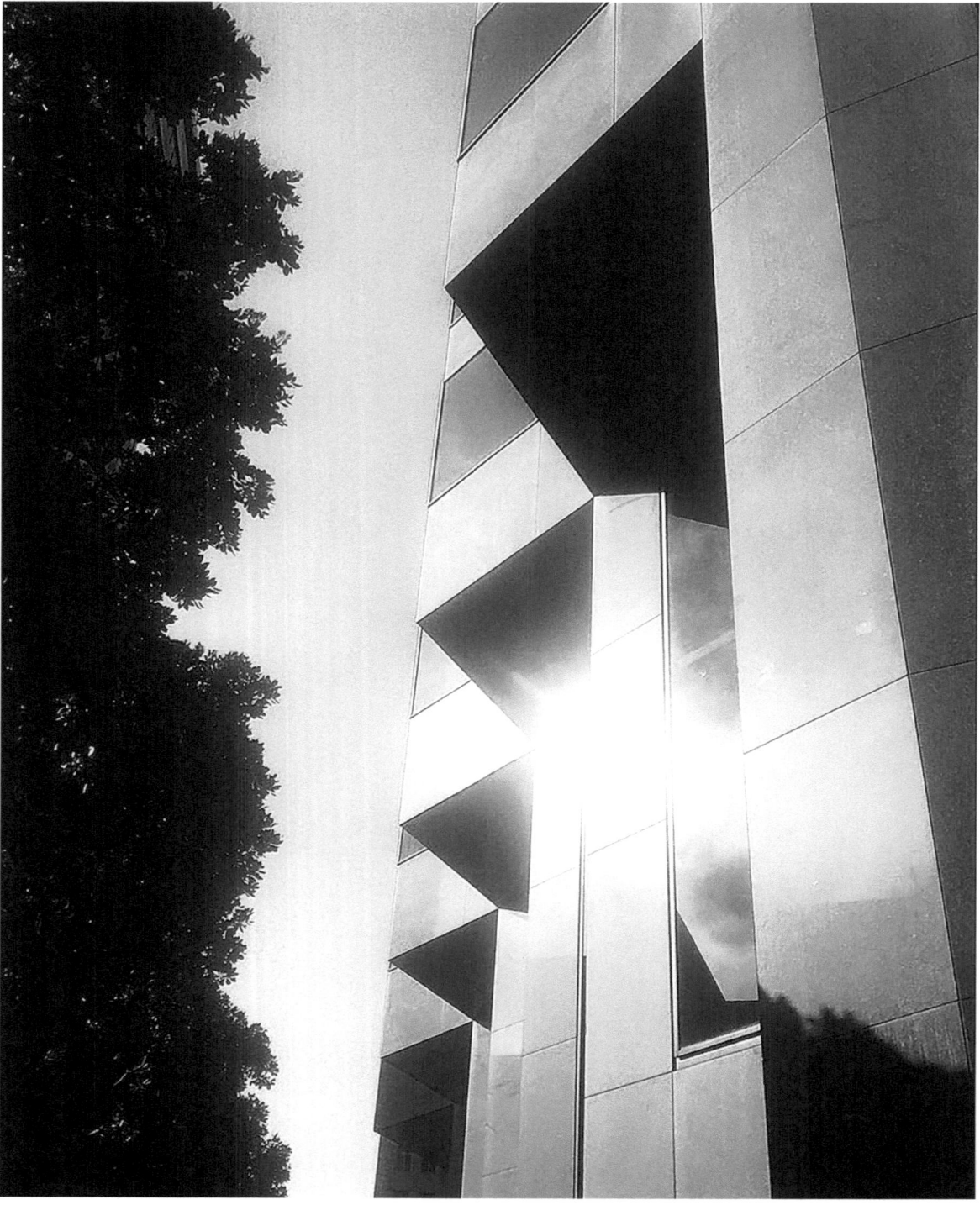

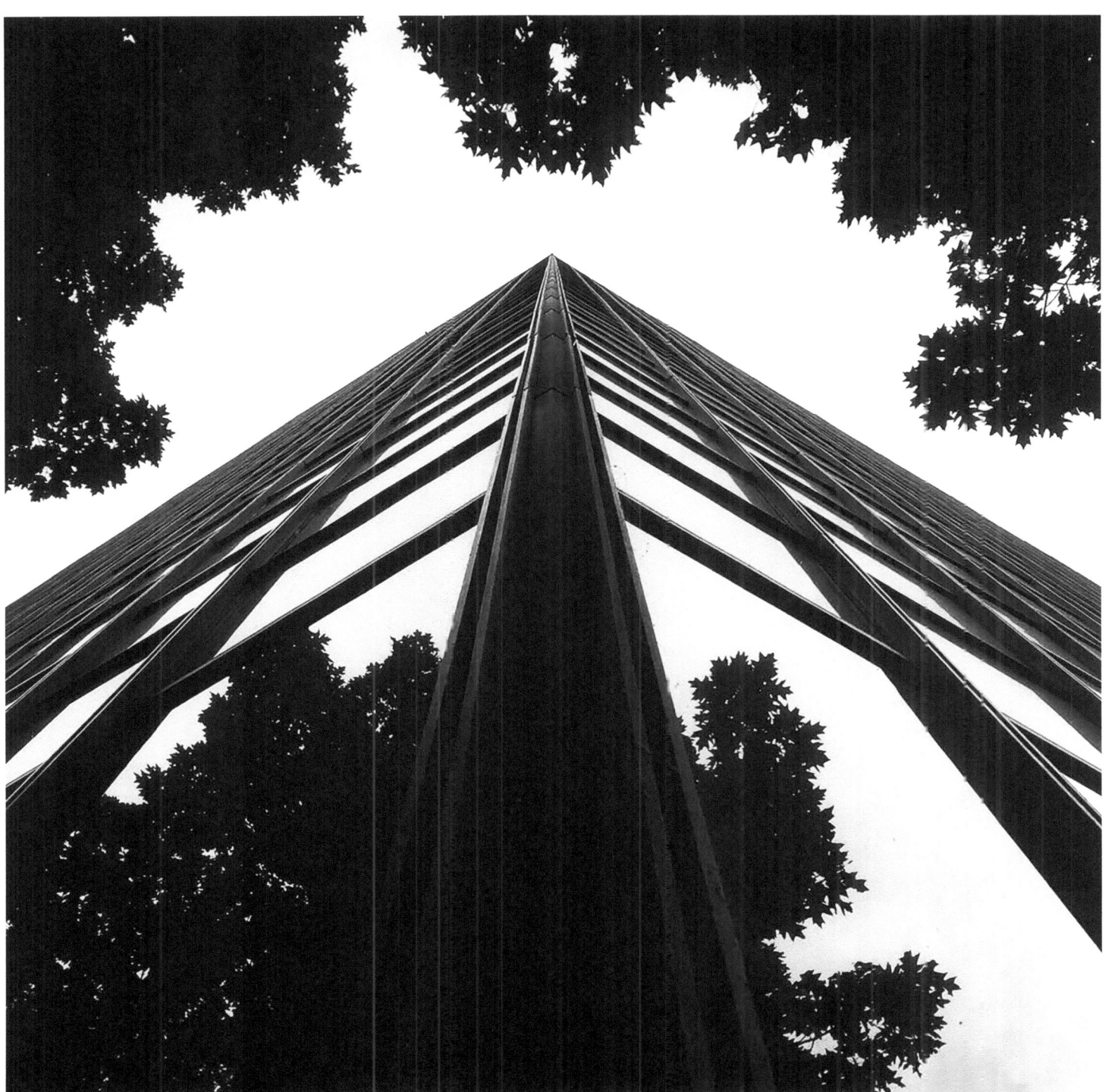

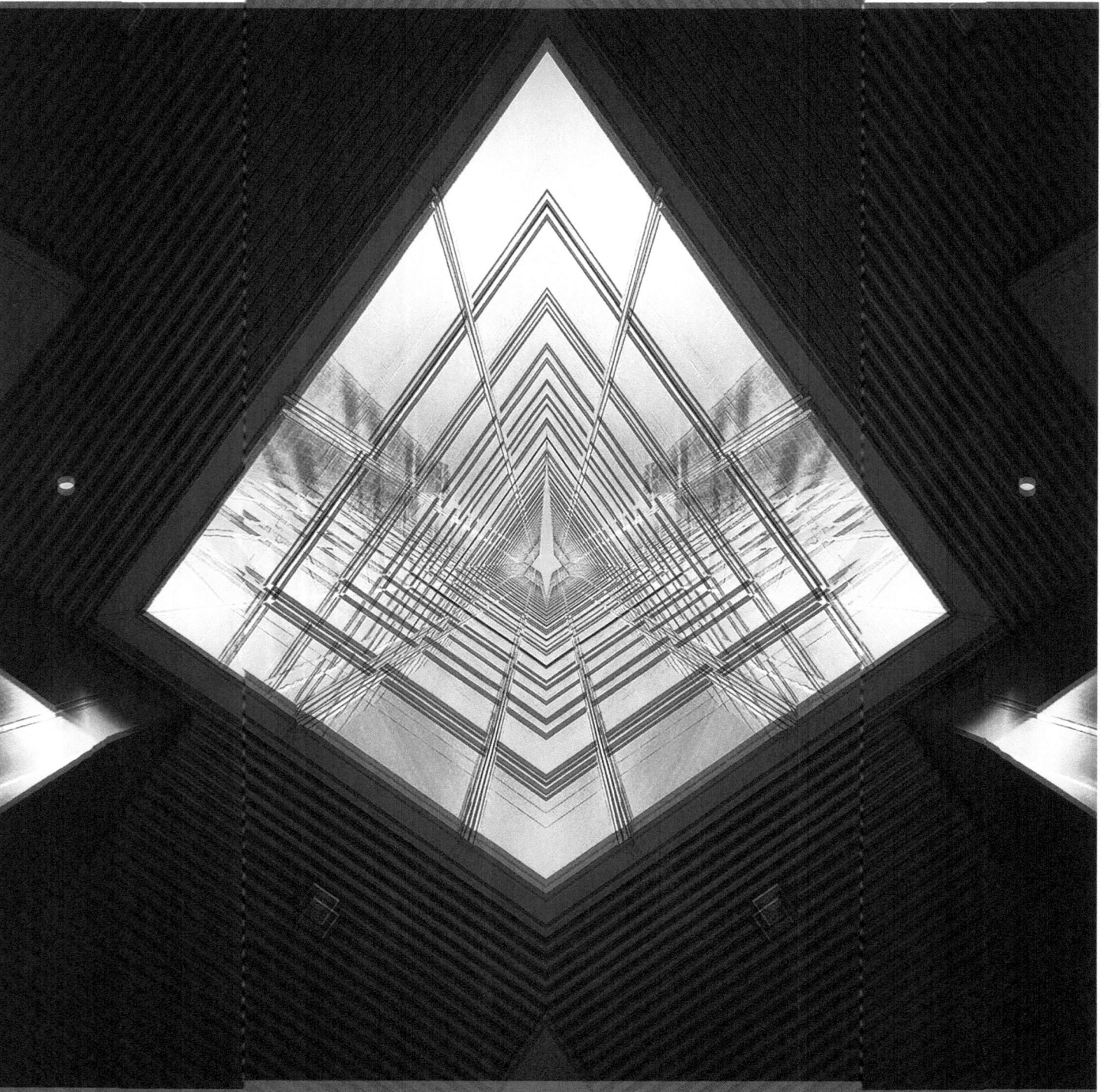

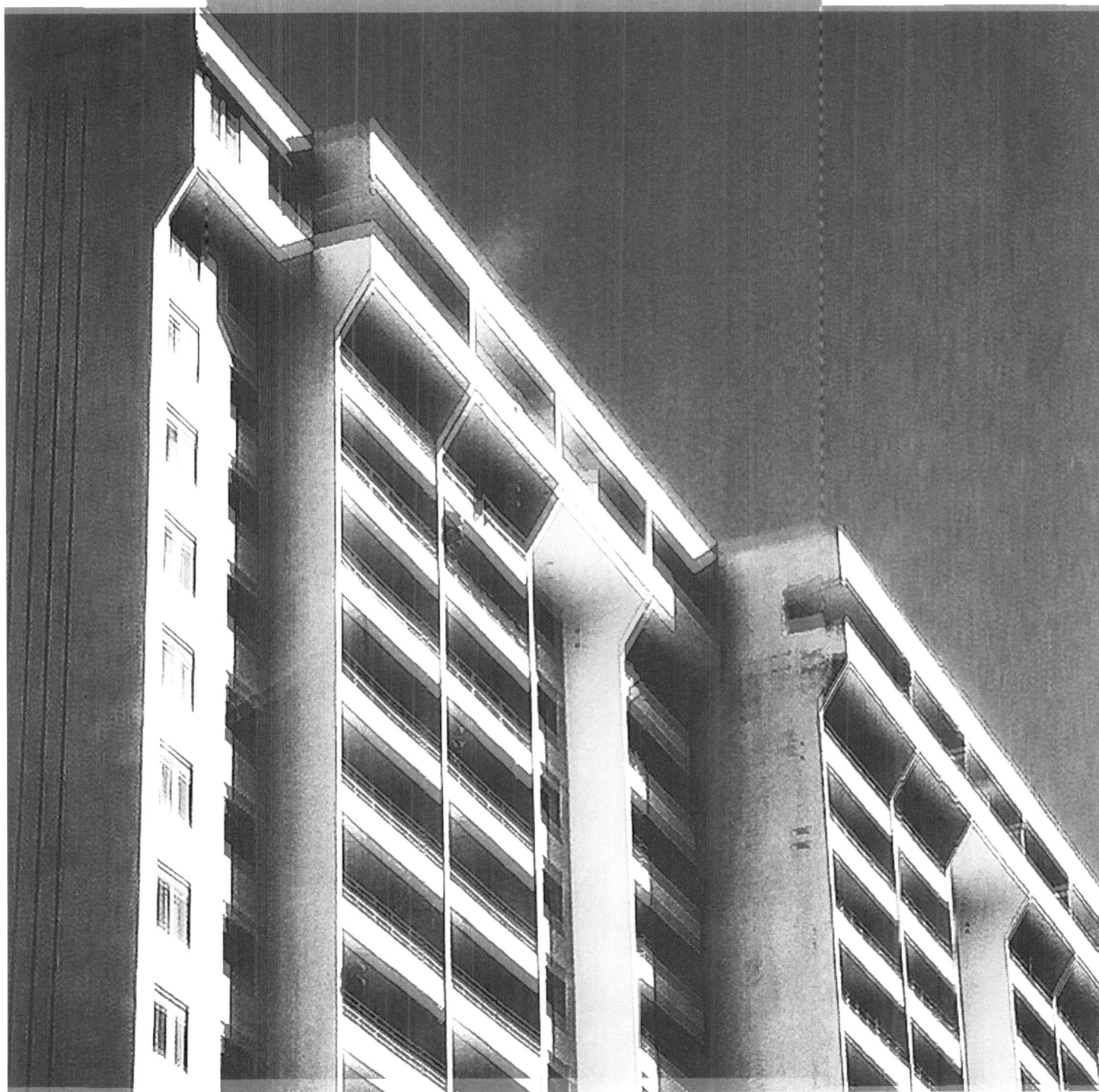

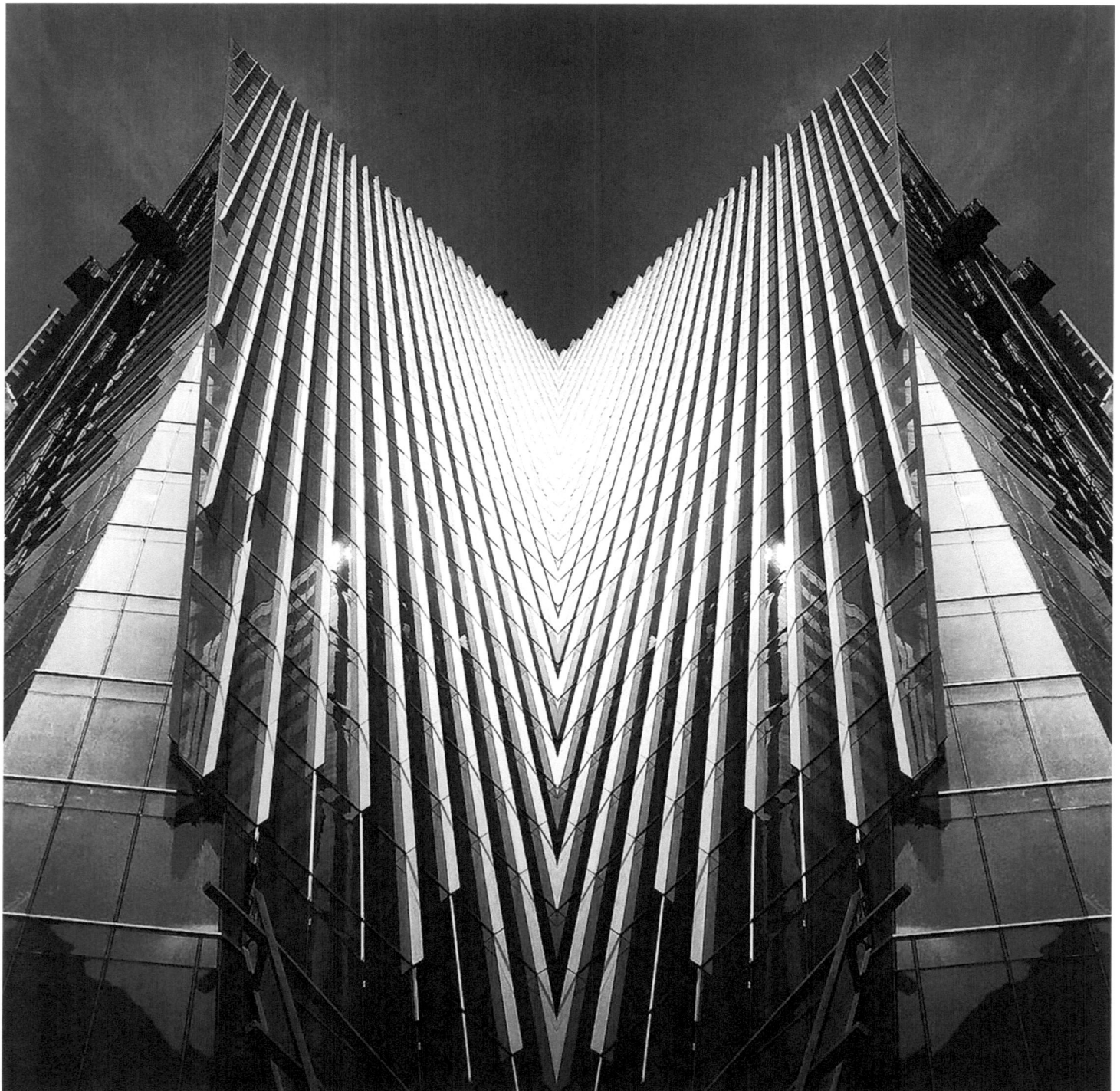

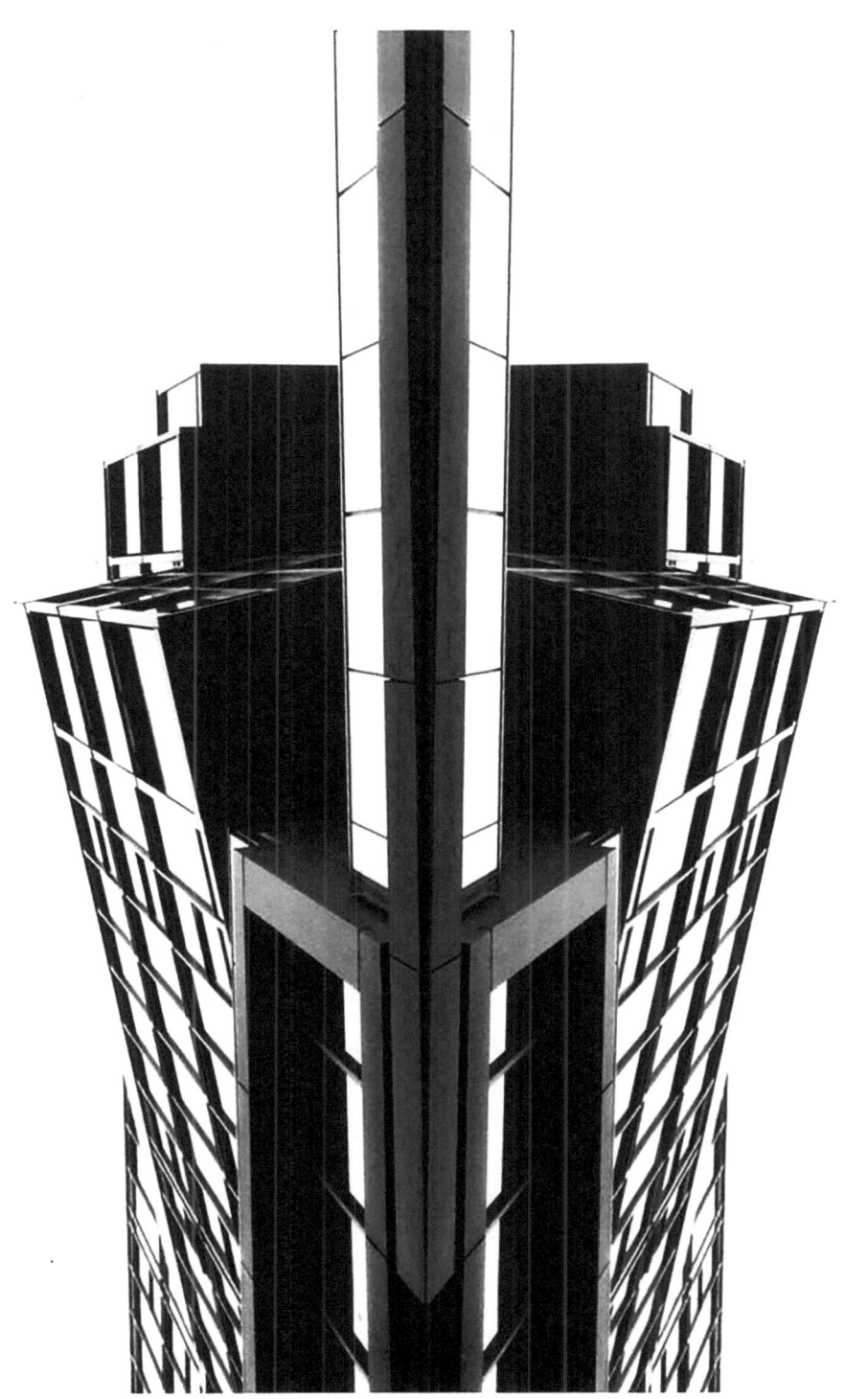

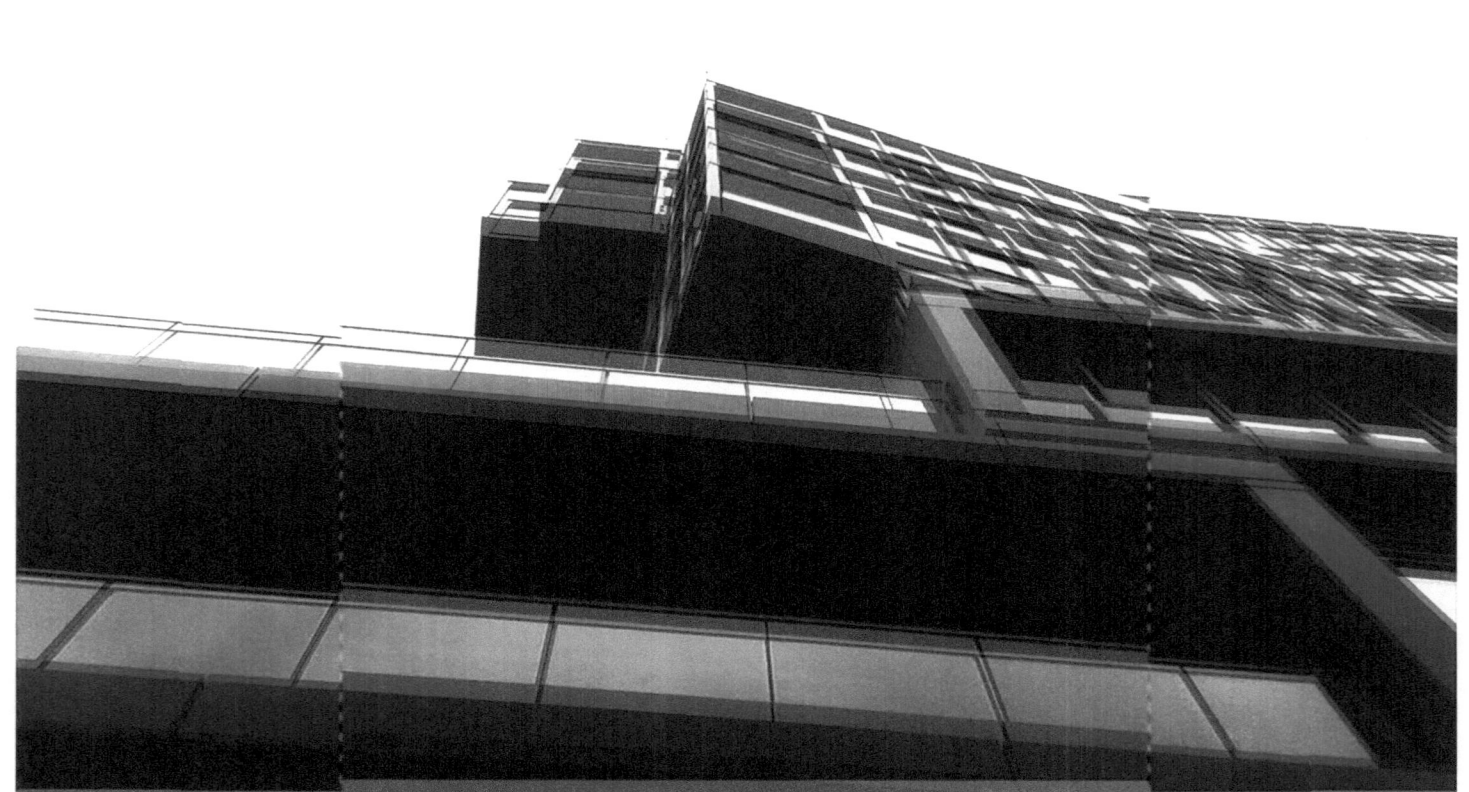

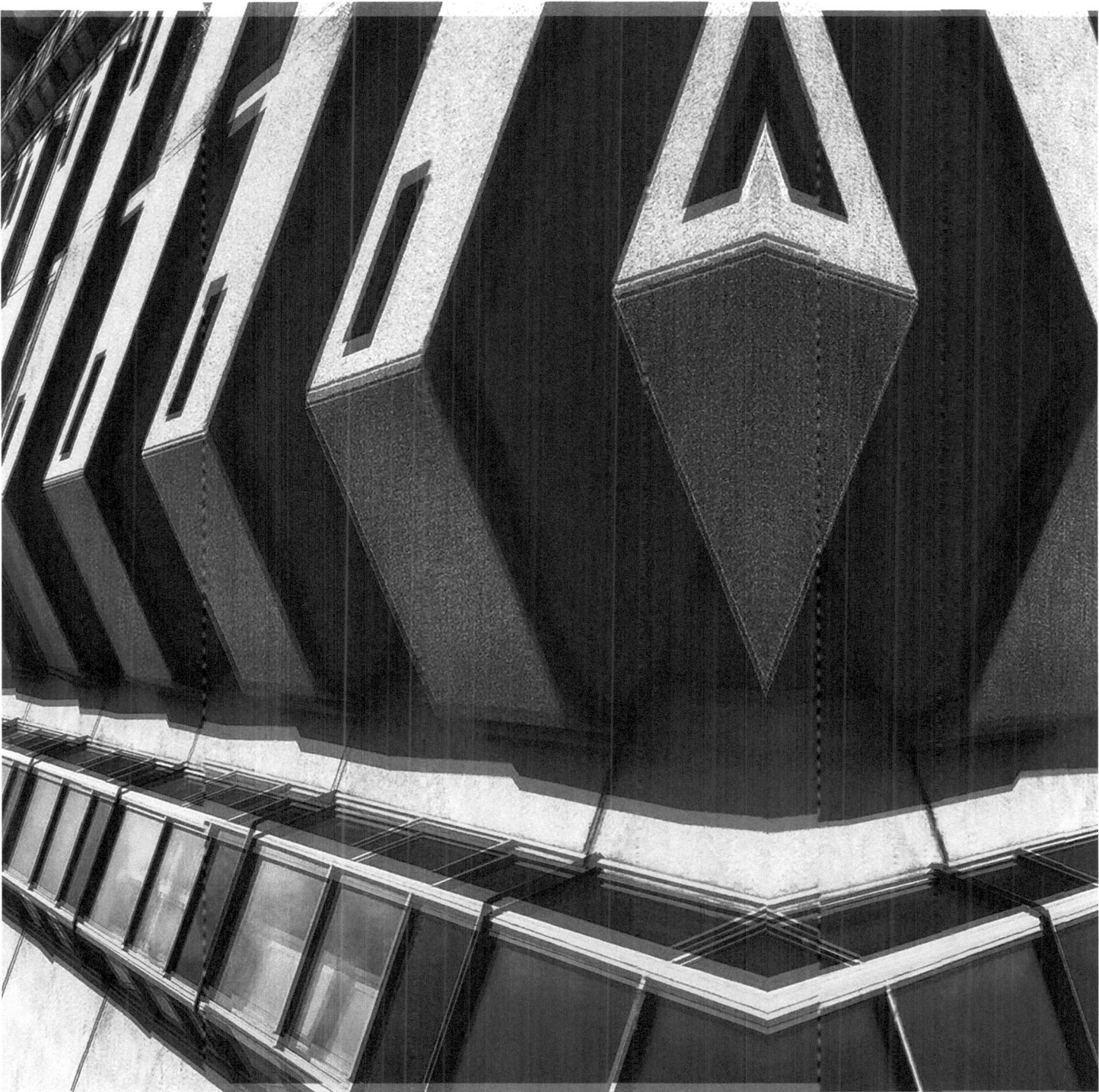

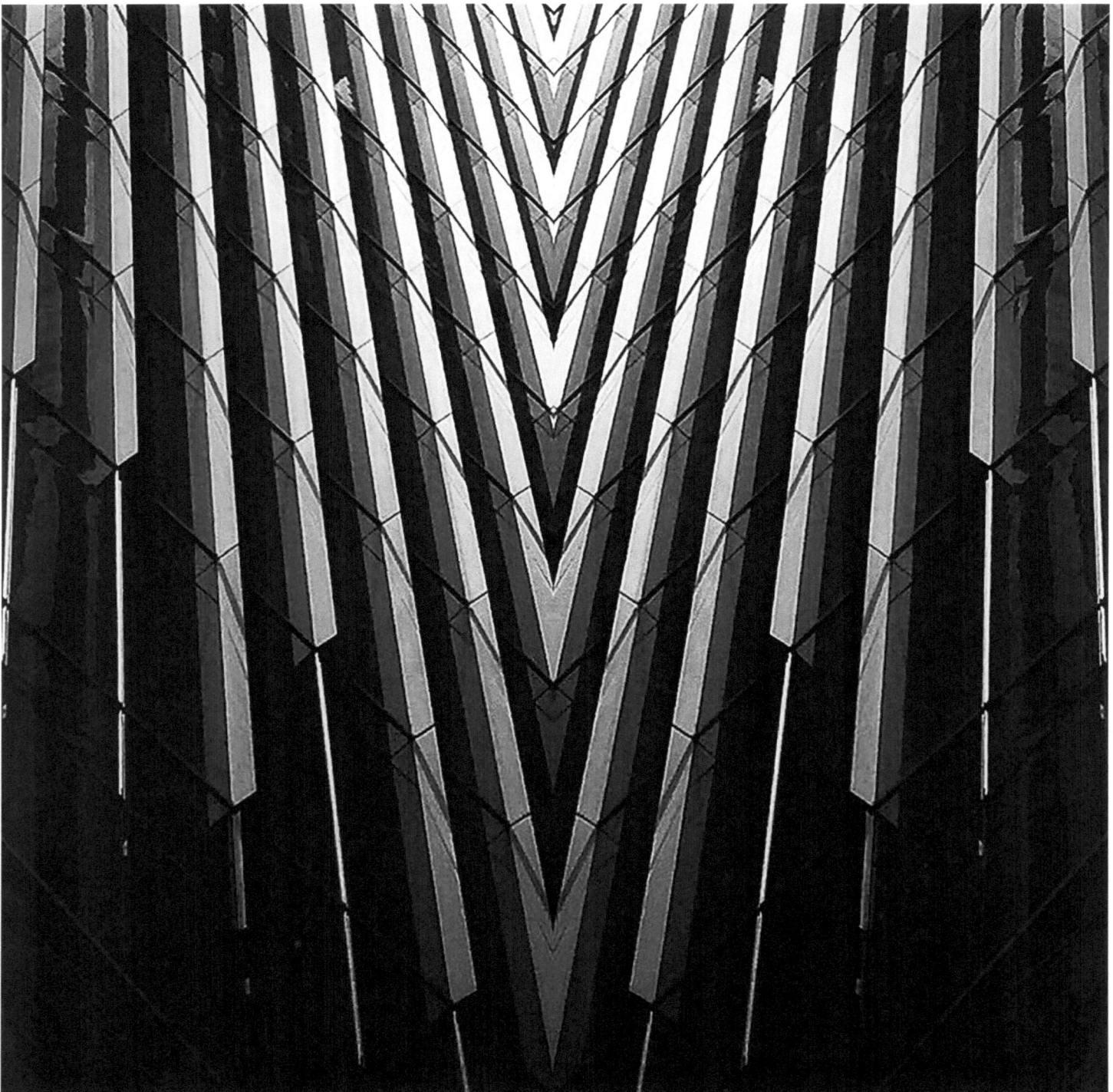

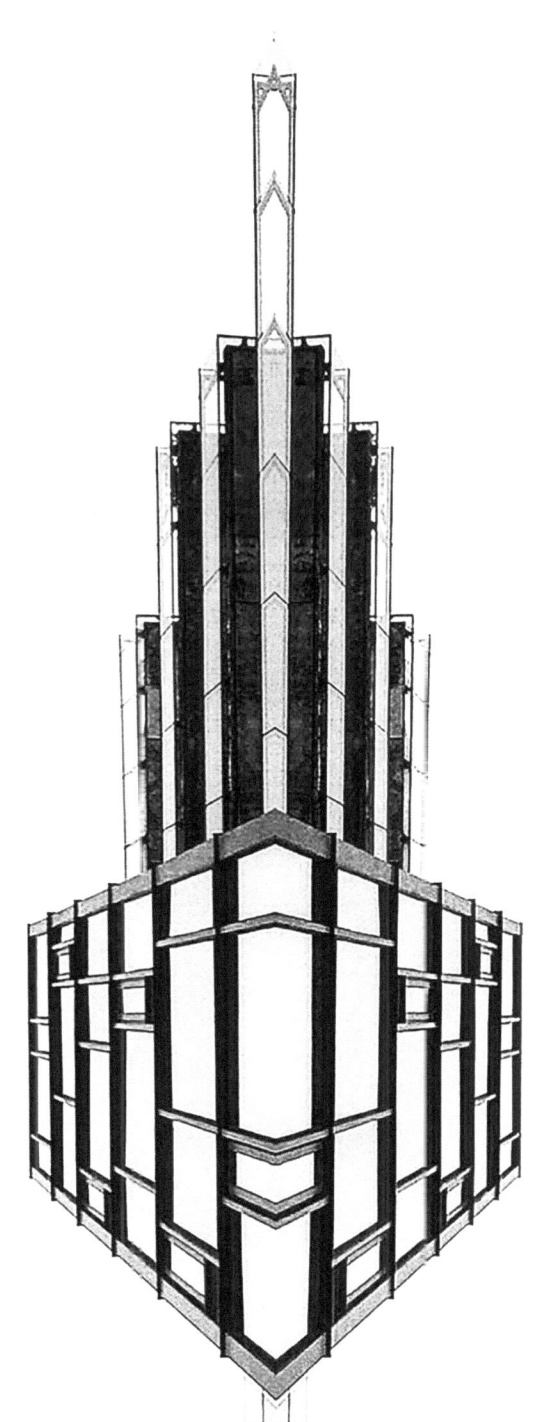

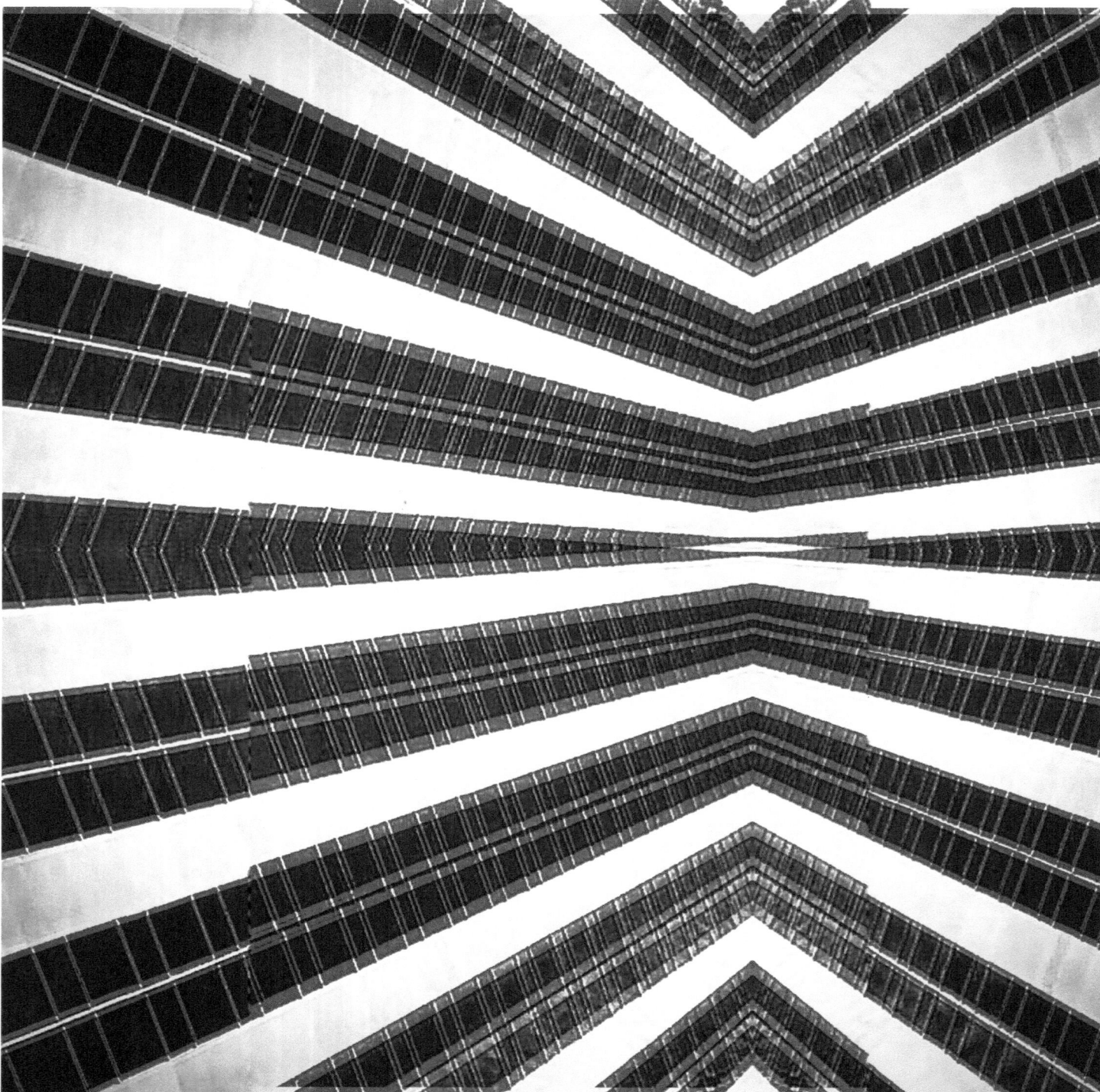

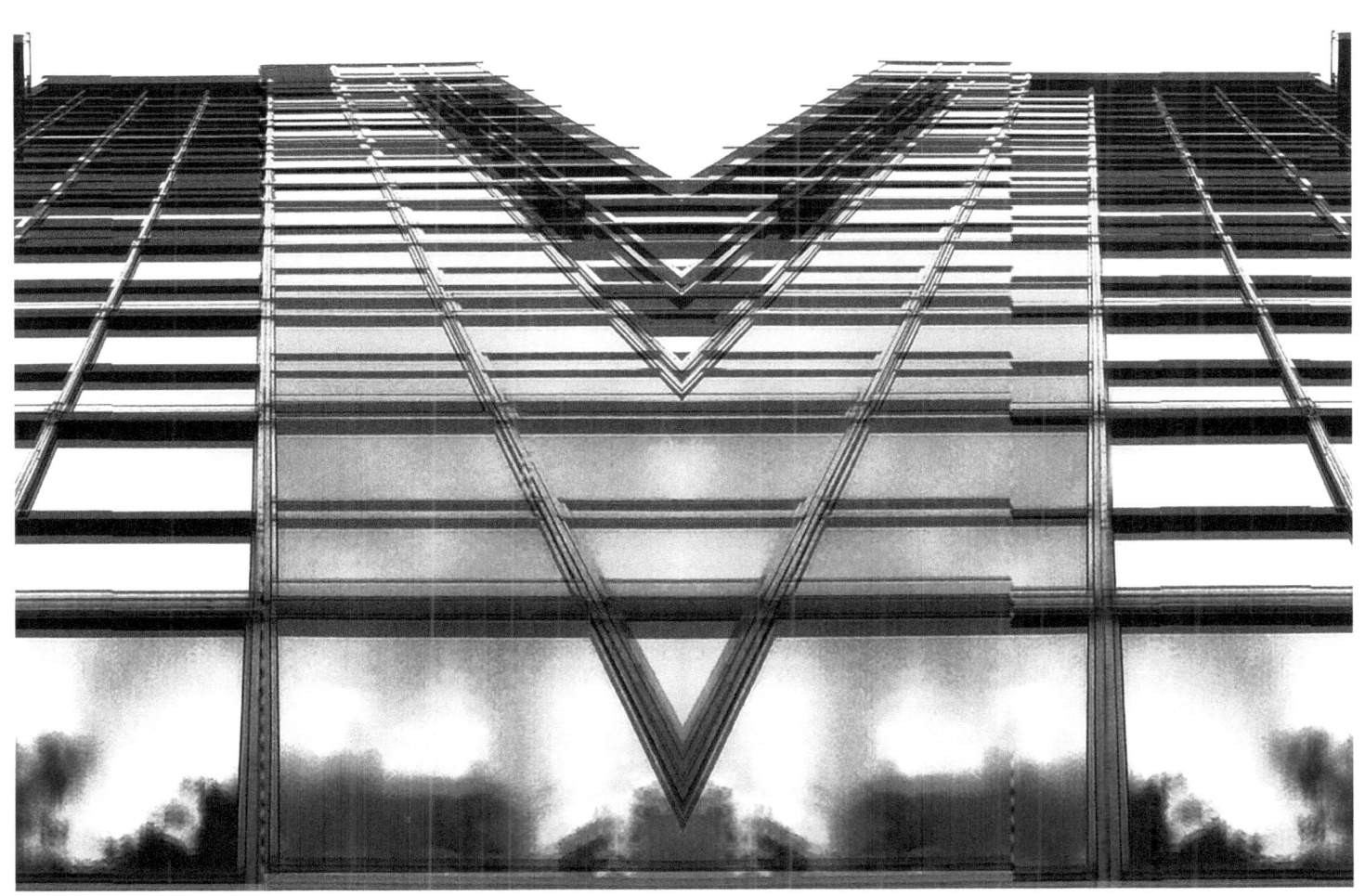

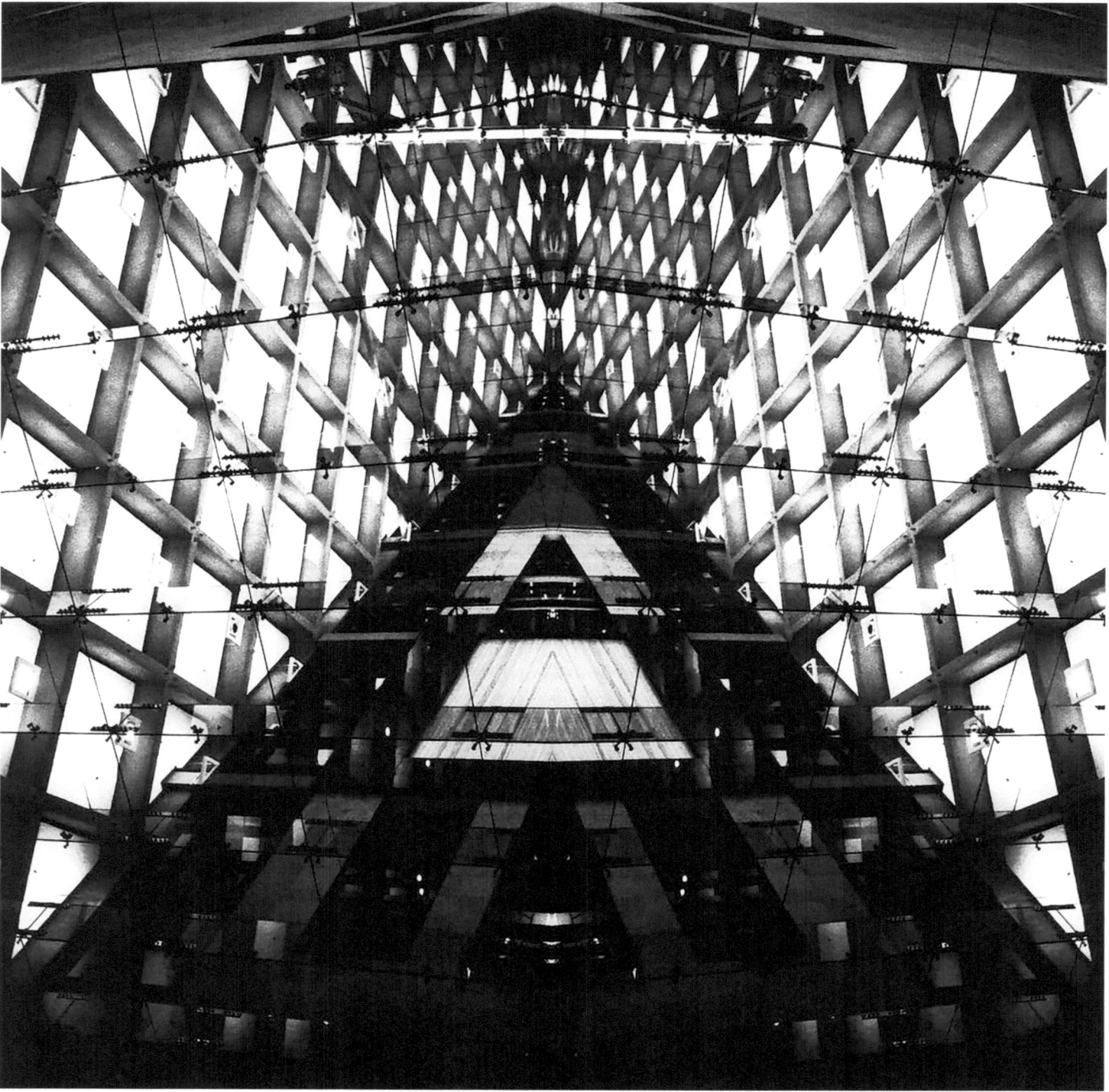

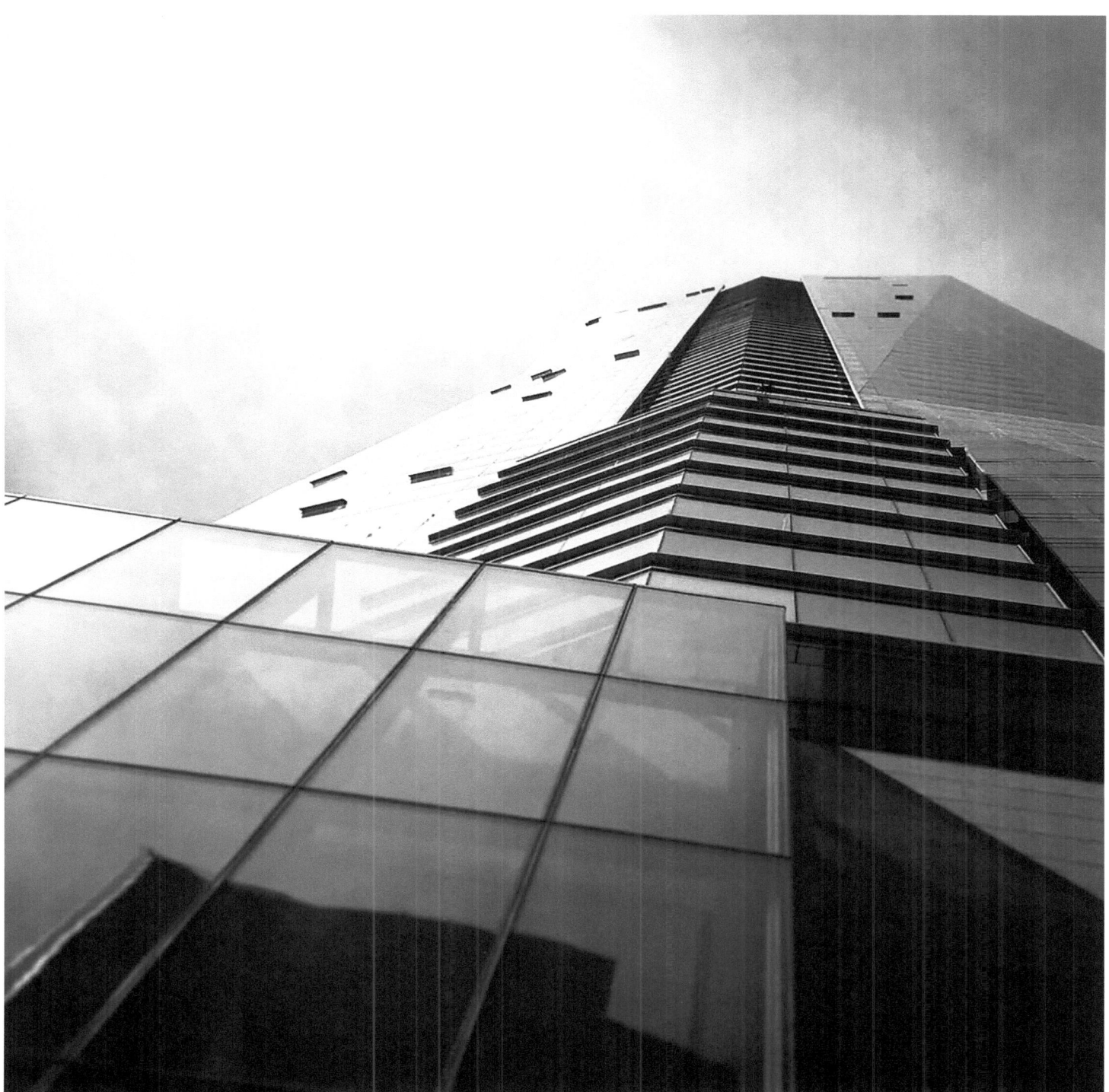

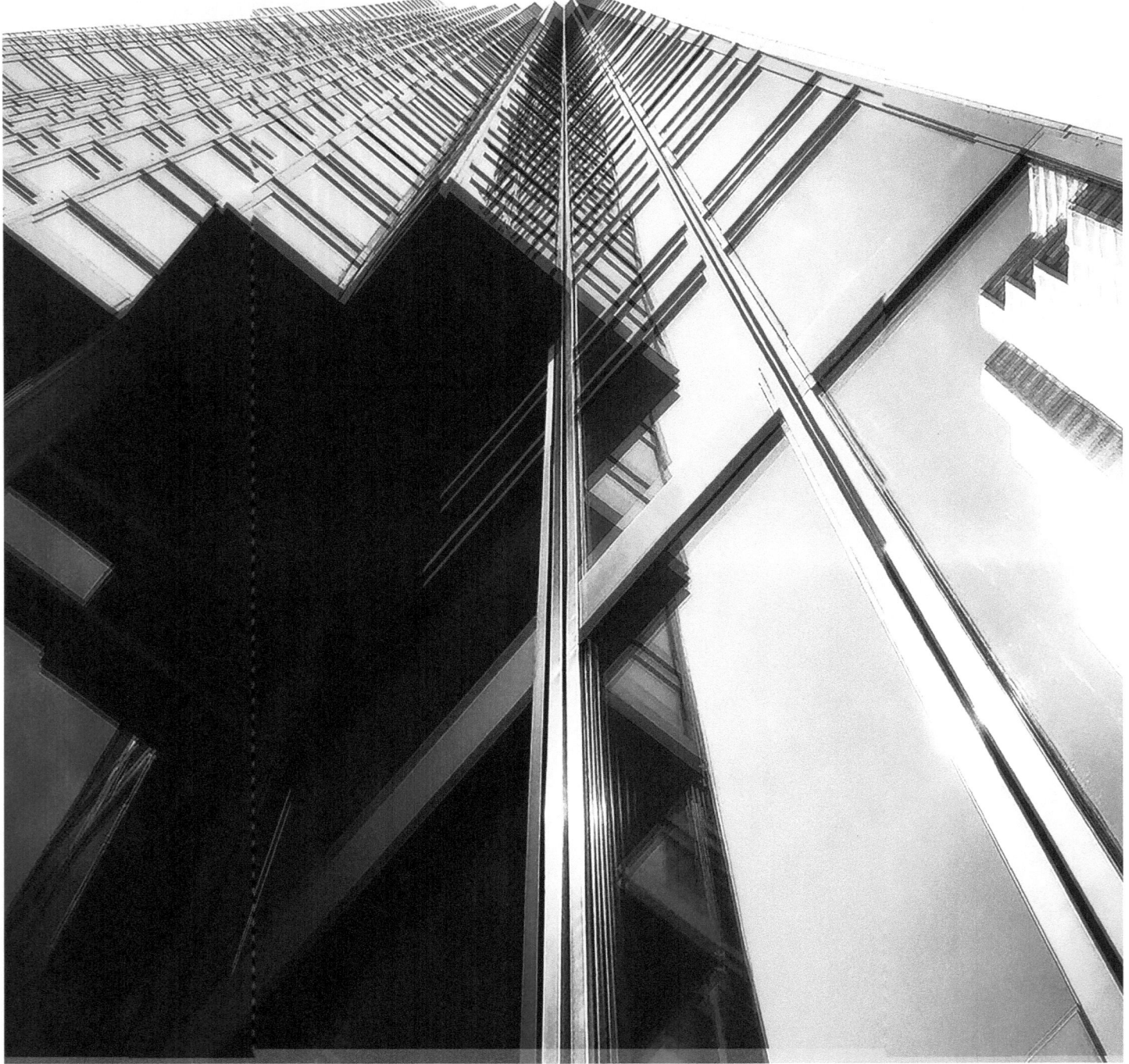

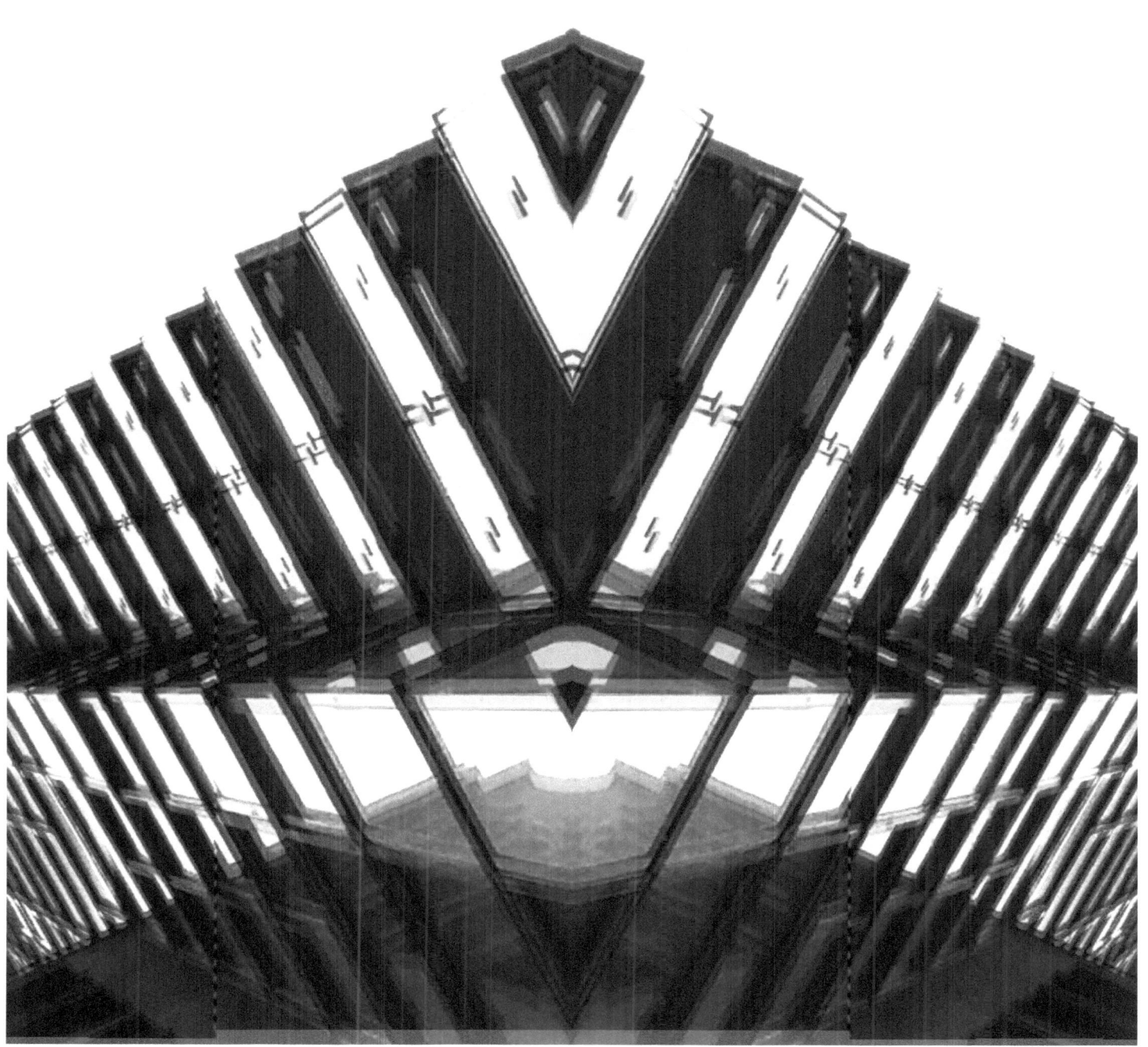

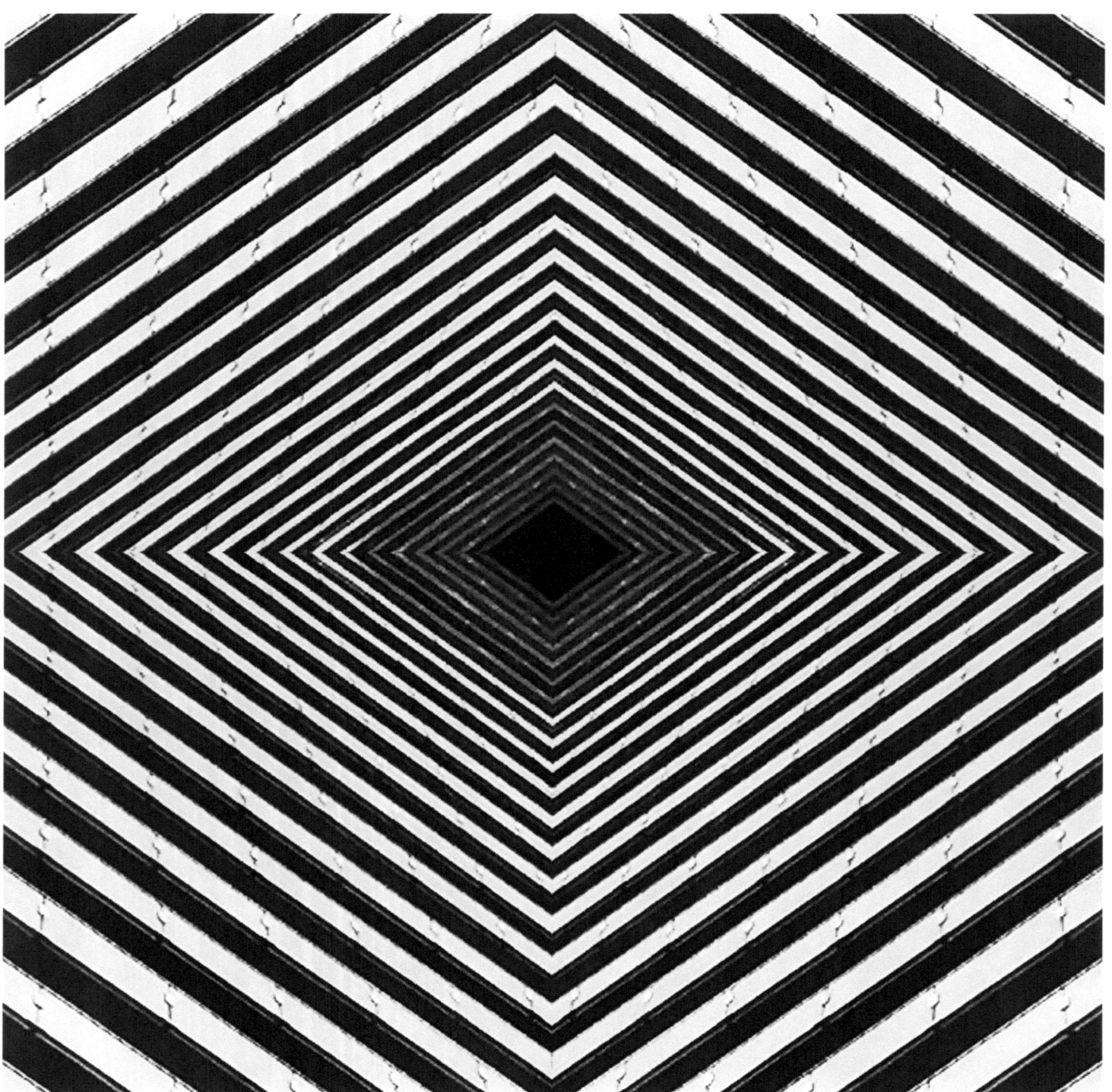

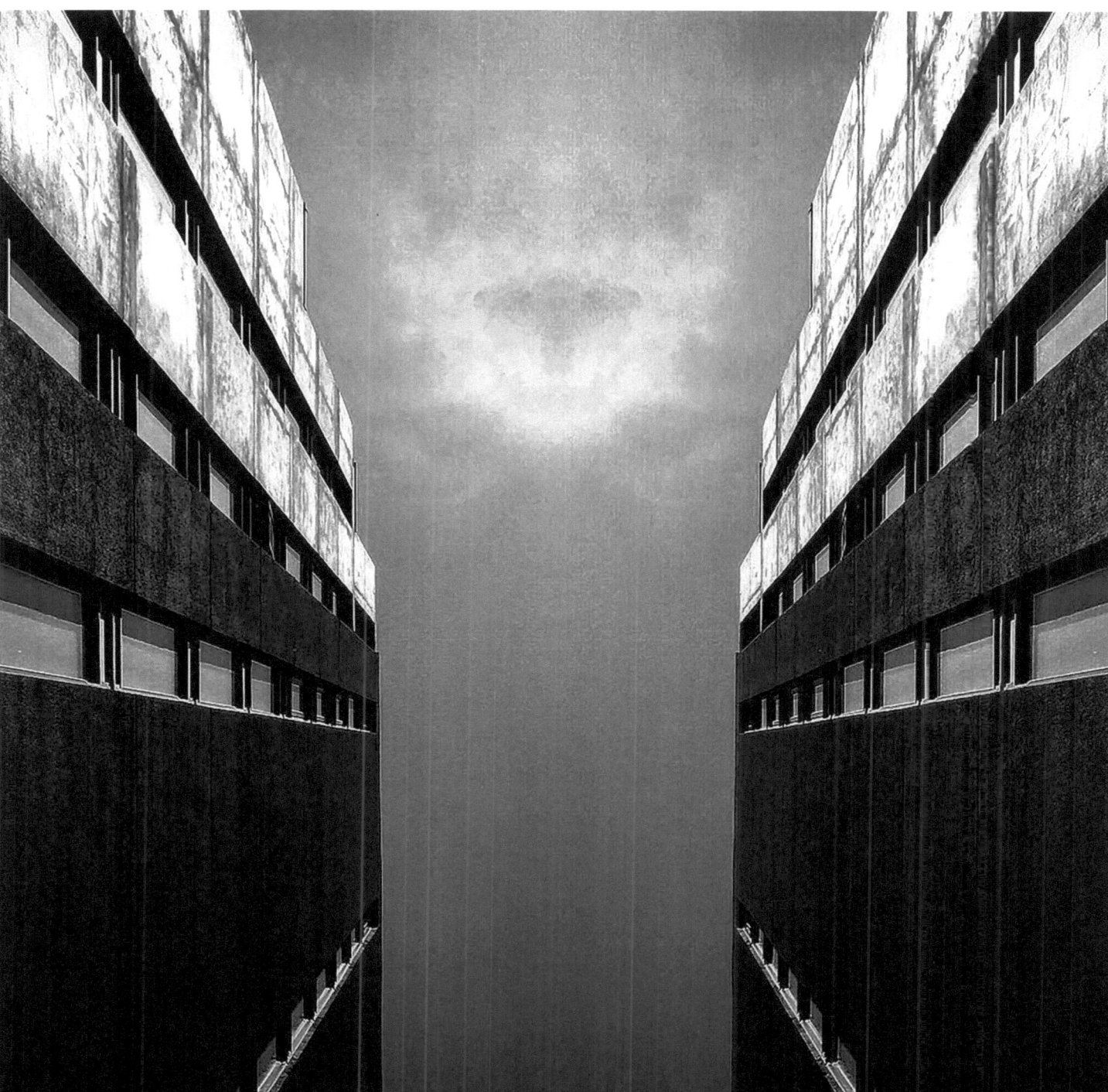

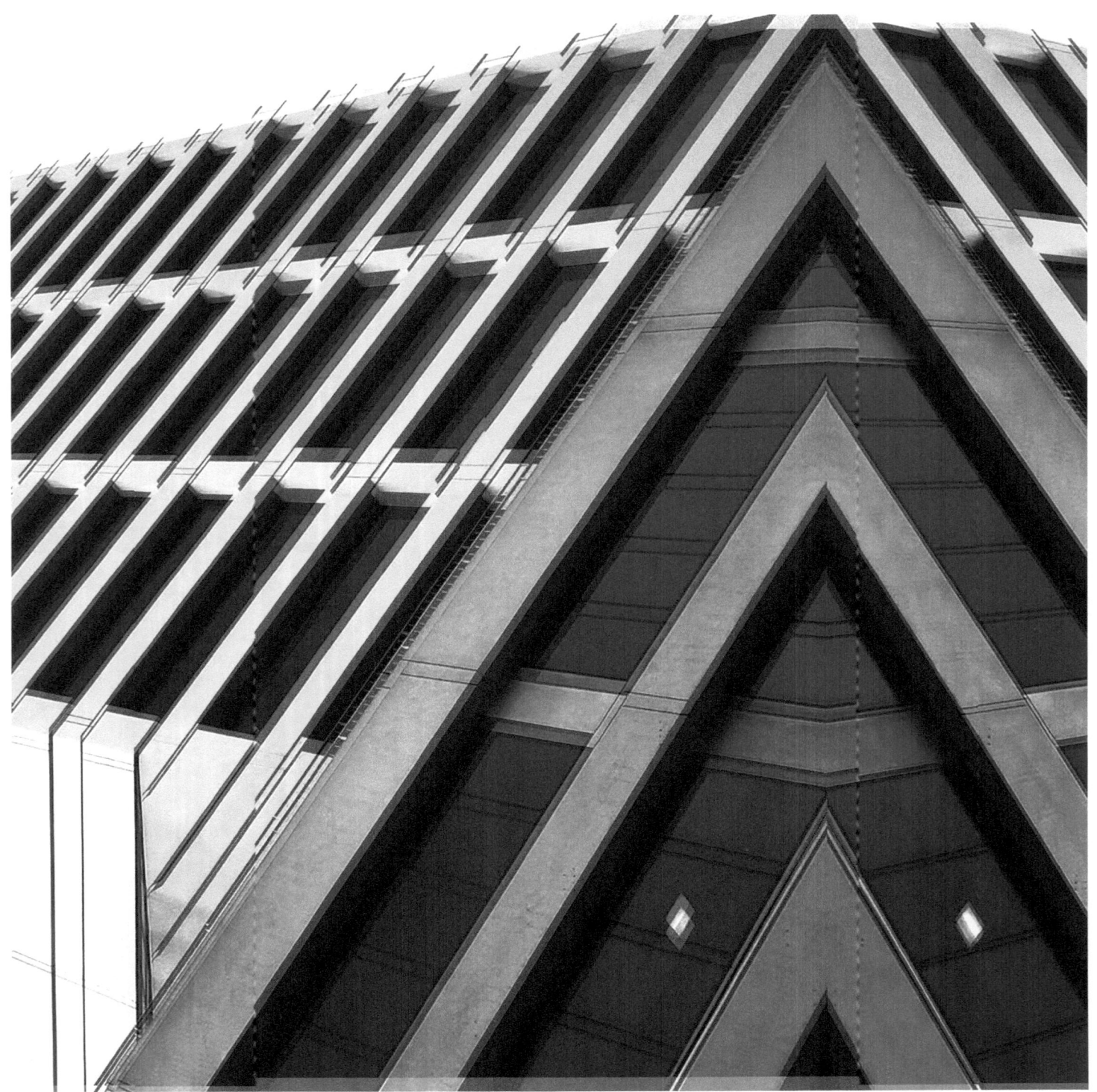

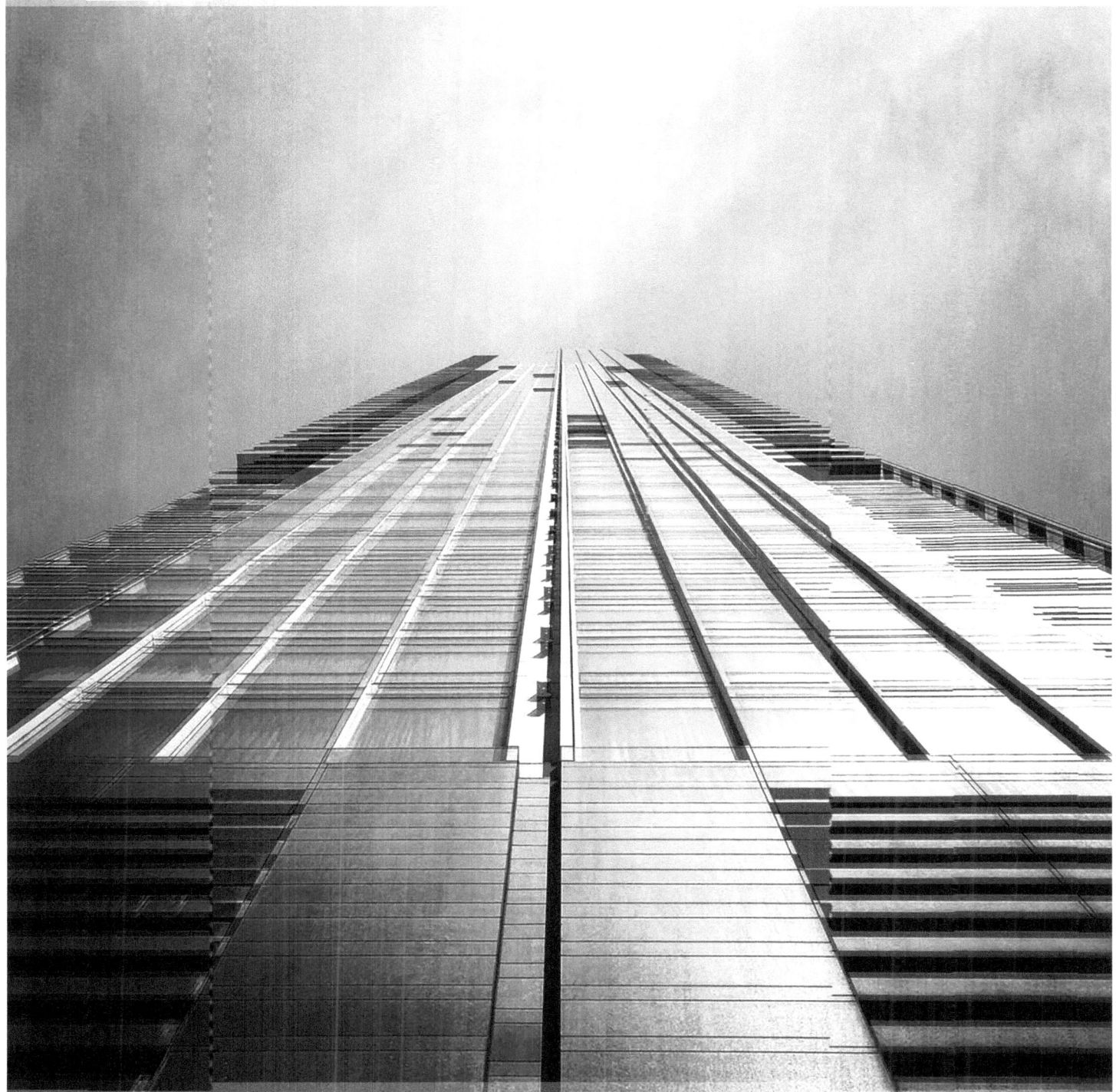

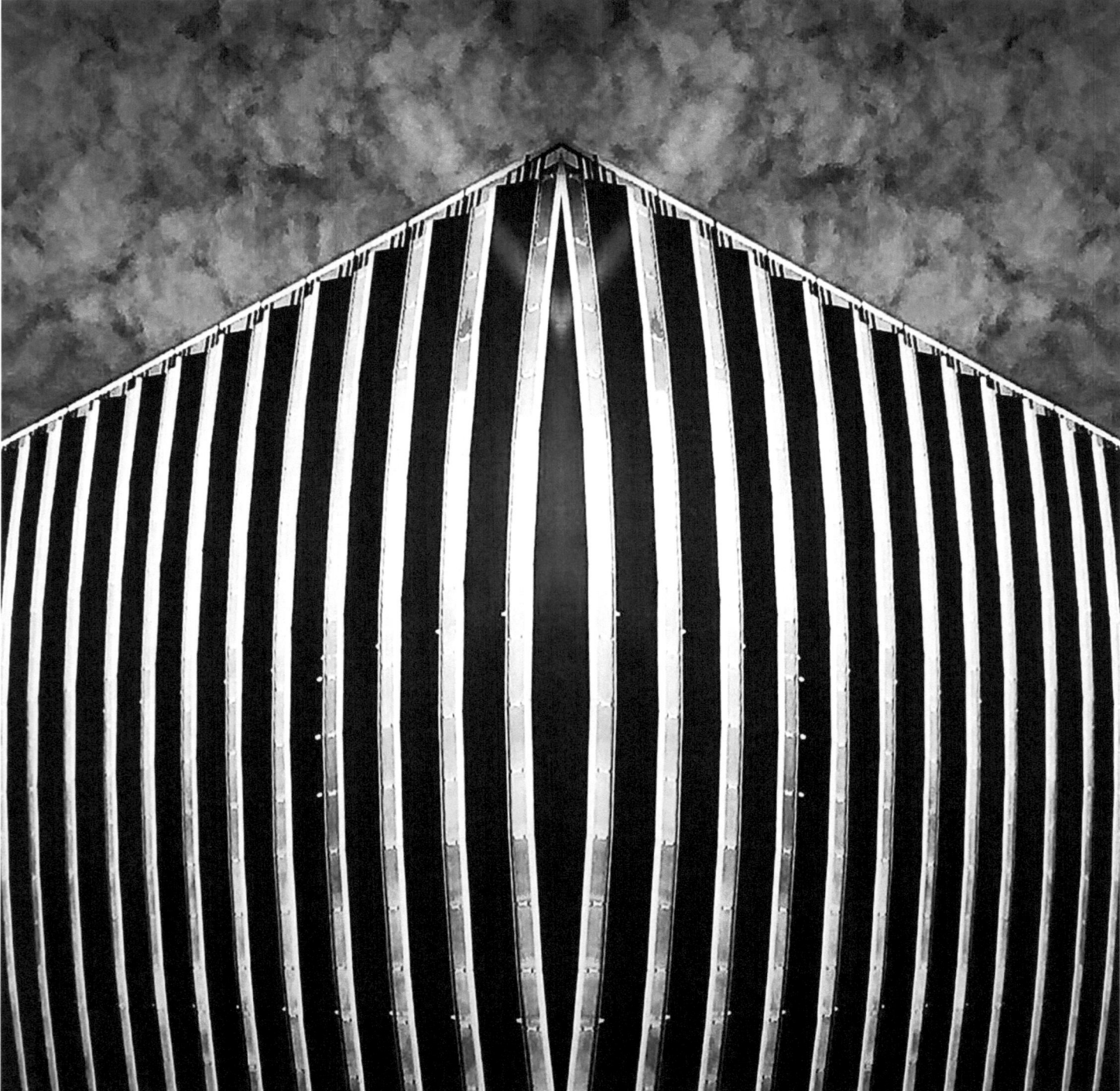

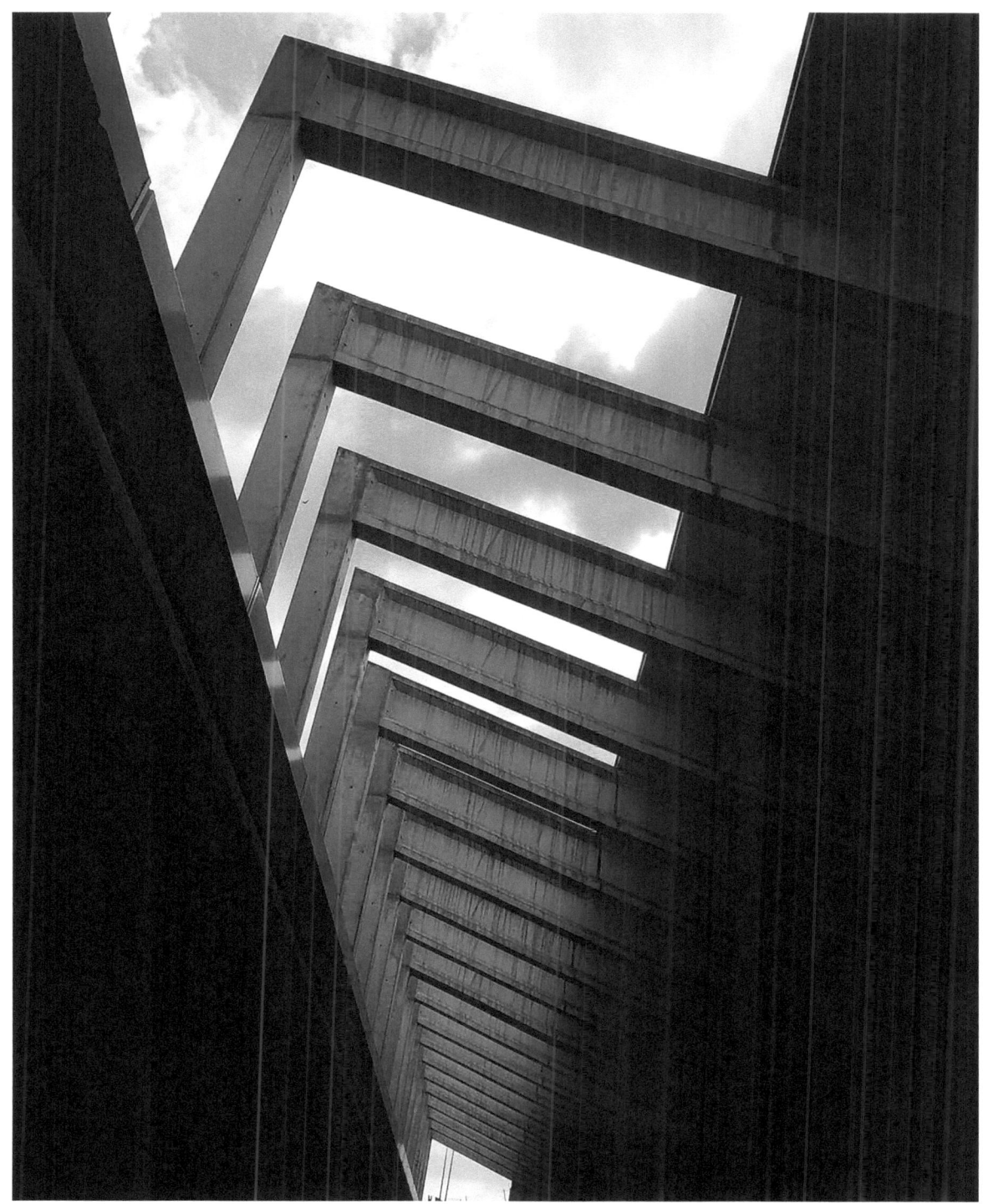

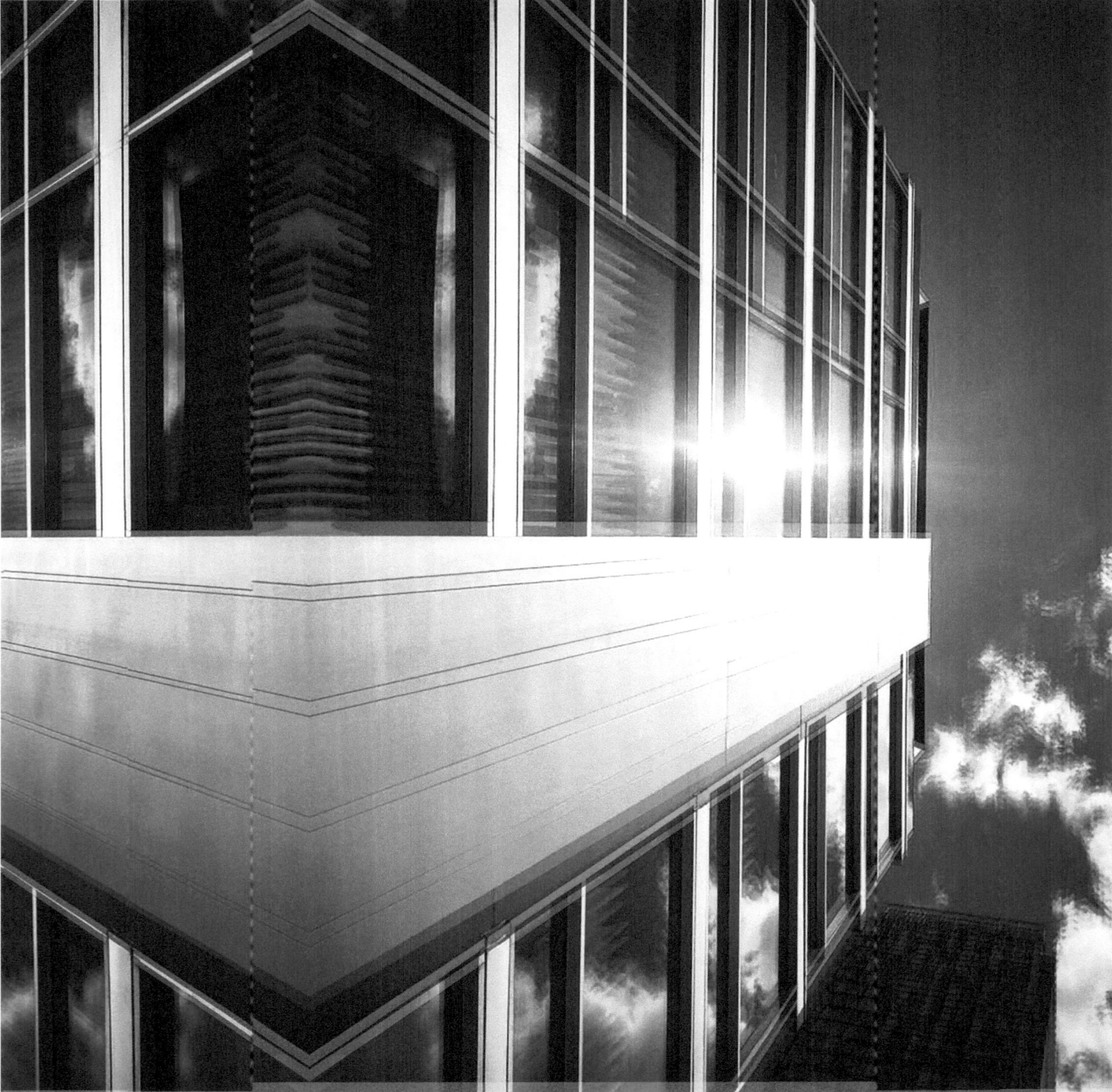

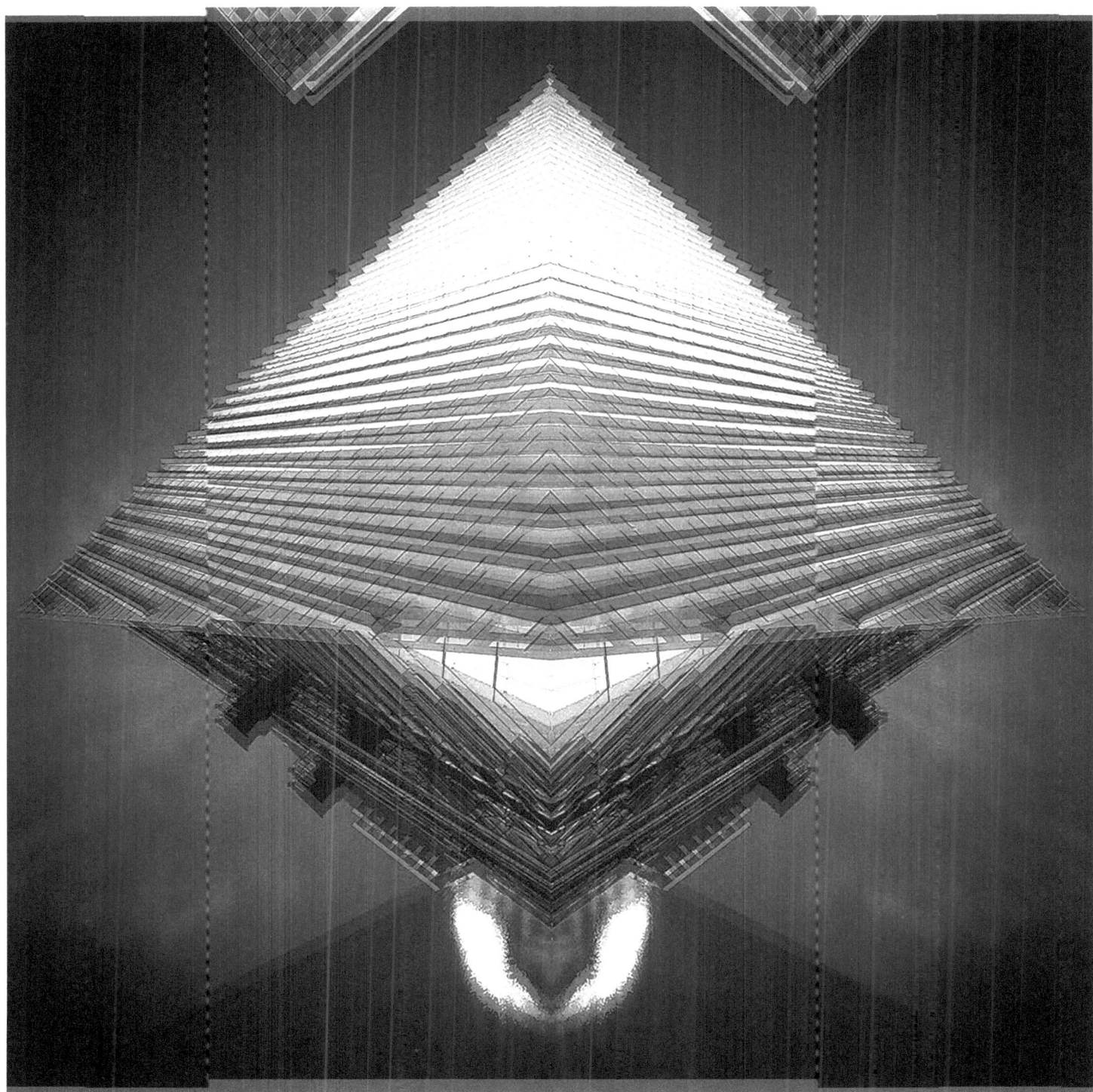

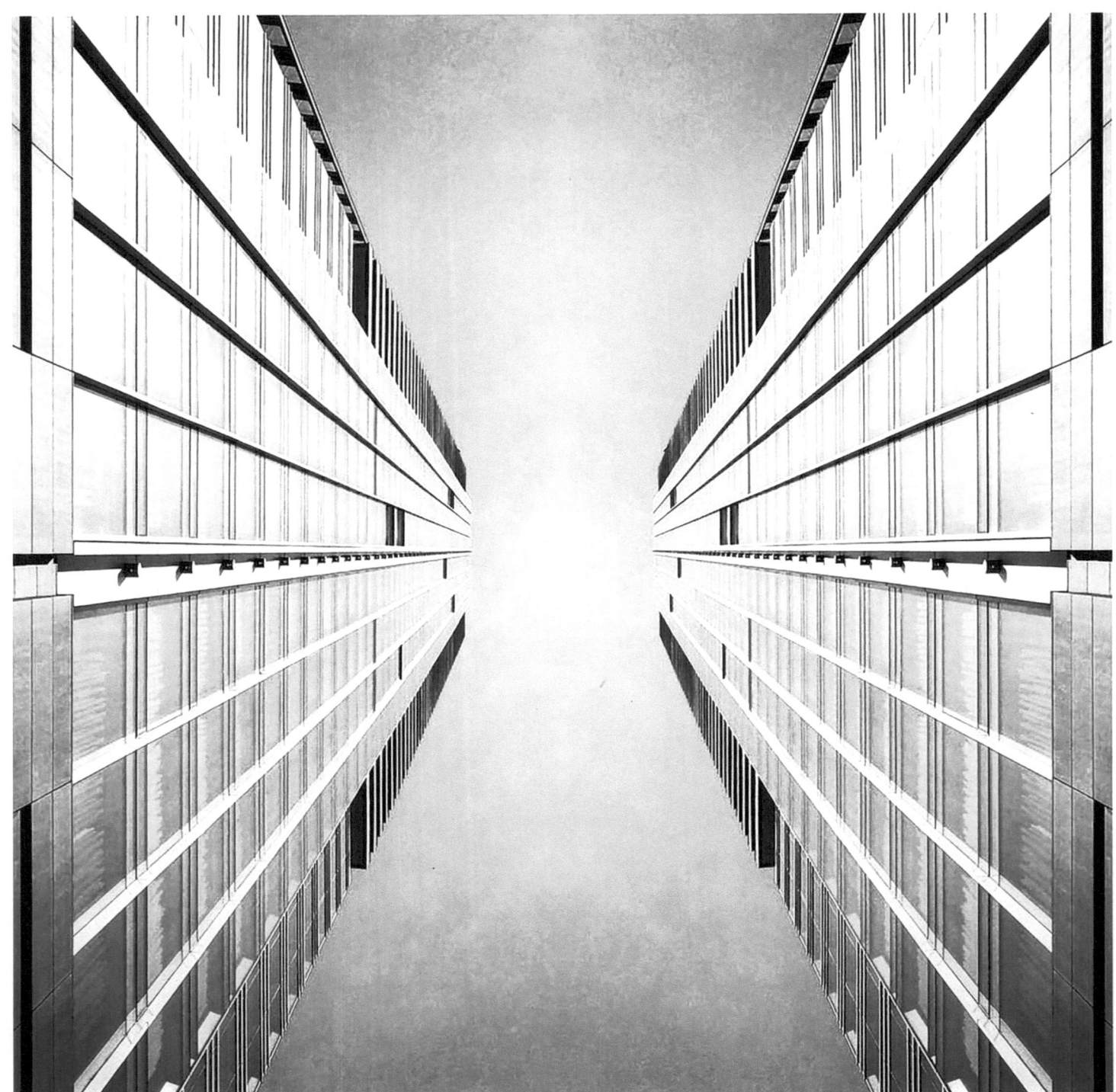

VERTEX
INDEX

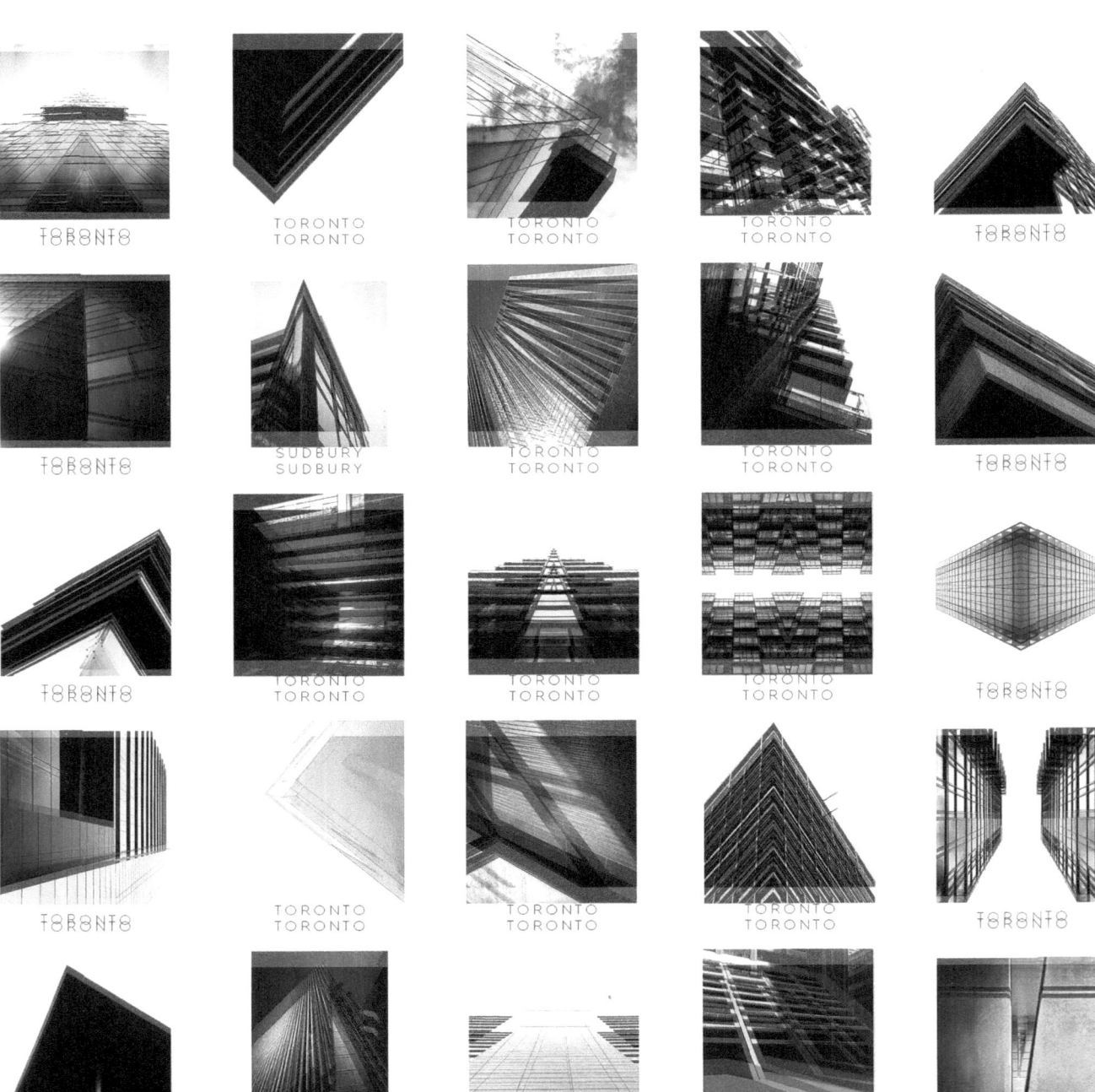

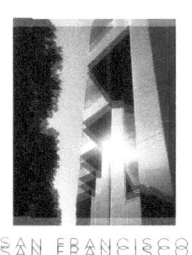 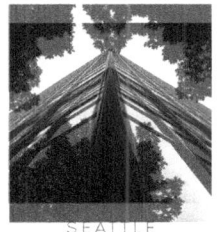 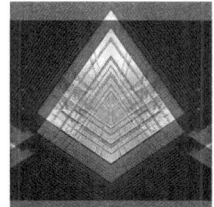 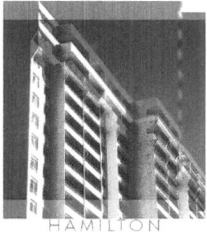 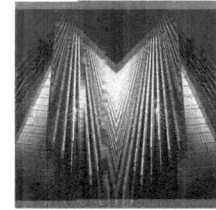

SAN FRANCISCO	SEATTLE	TORONTO	HAMILTON	TORONTO

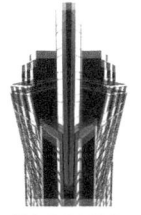 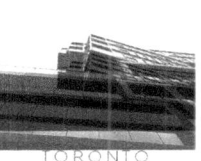 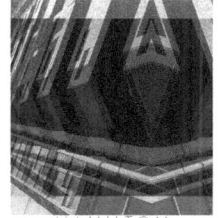 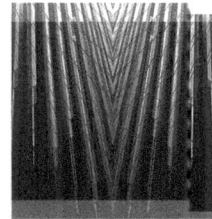 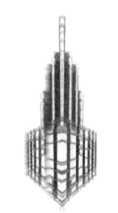

TORONTO	TORONTO	HAMILTON	TORONTO	TORONTO

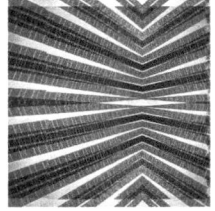 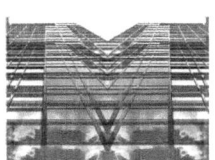 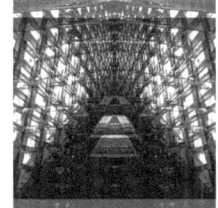 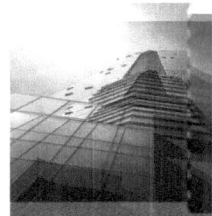 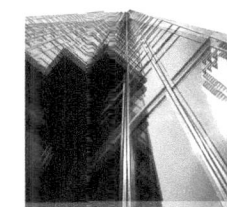

TORONTO	TORONTO	MONTREAL	TORONTO	TORONTO

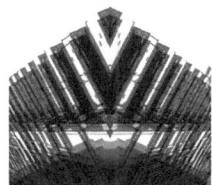 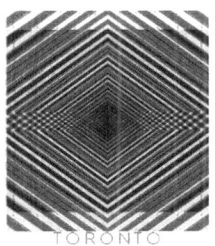 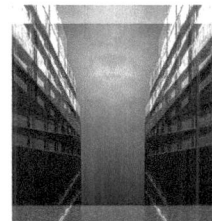 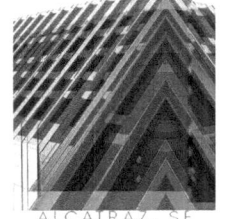 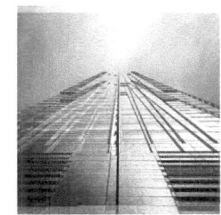

TORONTO	TORONTO	TORONTO	ALCATRAZ, SF	TORONTO

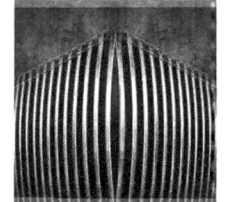 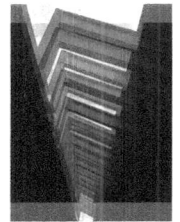 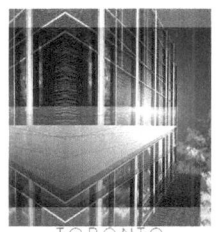 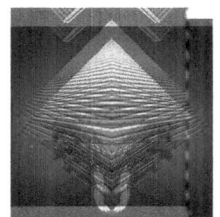 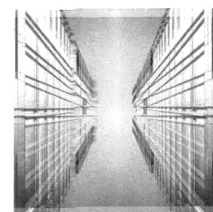

TORONTO	PARIS	TORONTO	TORONTO	TORONTO

www.ingramcontent.com/pod-product-compliance
Lightning Source LLC
Chambersburg PA
CBHW051921210526
45473CB00006B/2094